HIDING
FROM THE
SCHOOL
BUS

BREAKING FREE FROM
CONTROL, FEAR,
ISOLATION AND
A CHILDHOOD
WITHOUT EDUCATION

CALVIN BAGLEY

LEGACY
launch pad
PUBLISHING

ISBN: [978-1-964377-81-0] (ebook)

ISBN: [978-1-964377-87-2] (paperback)

ISBN: [978-1-964377-88-9] (hardcover)

Disclaimer

This book is a work of memory. While the events described are true to the author's recollection, some names, locations, and identifying characteristics have been changed to protect the privacy of those involved. Conversations and dialogue have been reconstructed to the best of the author's ability. In some instances, minor details and the timing of events have been compressed or reordered for narrative purposes.

For Karissa, Christian and Victoria —
You are the life I never thought I could have.

And to the boy who hid from the school bus —
you were always worth saving.

"The weight of this sad time we must obey. Speak what we feel, not what we ought to say."
—William Shakespeare, King Lear

"For my part, I consider that it will be found much better by all parties to leave the past to history, especially as I propose to write that history myself."
—Winston Churchill

ADVANCE PRAISE

PRAISE FOR CALVIN BAGLEY AND *HIDING FROM THE SCHOOL BUS*

"I've had the privilege of knowing Calvin Bagley through Genius Network, and he embodies everything I believe about transforming pain into purpose. Calvin didn't just overcome a traumatic childhood—he used those experiences to build a multi-million-dollar business based on genuine care and doing the right thing, even when it costs money. He's proof that where you come from doesn't determine where you can go, and he's the kind of person who makes you believe in the power of the human spirit."

—Joe Polish, Genius Network and Genius Recovery, and *Wall Street Journal* bestselling author of *What's In It For Them: 9 Genius Networking Principles to Get What You Want by Helping Others Get What They Want*

"I got to know Calvin through working with him as a client, and over time, he became a friend—but reading *Hiding from the School Bus* shook me. I had no idea of the pain he lived

through, the isolation he endured or the silent battles he fought as a child. This memoir isn't just powerful—it's heartbreaking and courageous. Calvin shares, with raw vulnerability, what it's like to grow up hidden from the world, denied an education and silenced by fear. But through every page, you witness the fire that refused to go out. This is a story of reclaiming your voice, rewriting your story and proving that even the most broken beginnings don't get to define your ending. It's unforgettable.
5 STARS!!!!"

—Whitney Jones, three-time Ms. Fitness Olympia Champion

"To see who Calvin is, despite what he has suffered, is pure motivation. His life is a living testimony of these truths: purpose turns pain into muscle, and discomfort is the currency of heaven."

—Samuel Castor, author of *Zion Rising*

"Calvin doesn't just tell a story he opens a door. What he walked through in silence he now shares with courage, offering hope to every man still hiding from his own pain. This book is a bold reminder that healing begins when we stop running and finally face the truth."

—Ryan James Miller, performance coach and author

"Sometimes the road less traveled is the one that leads us home to ourselves. Calvin Bagley's story is about more than over-coming—it's about becoming. He shows us that our scars don't define us, but how we choose to heal them does."

—Kimberly Shannon Murphy, stuntwoman and author of *Glimmer: A Story of Survival, Hope, and Healing*

"Calvin Bagley went from an abusive, broken childhood to a holistically abundant adulthood. Within the pages, you will be surprised and emotional but also inspired. It will leave you knowing how you can elevate your life to the next level."

—Dr. Isaac H. Jones, founder and CEO of Centagio Hotels and founder of Health Experts Alliance

"Calvin doesn't just share his journey—he invites us into it. His courage, faith and grit make this a powerful read for anyone who's ever wondered if brokenness disqualifies them from making a difference."

—Dale R. Wills, owner/founder, real estate developer and home builder

"If you want to be inspired by how a person can transform a tremendously painful childhood into an emotionally rich adult life grounded in faith and love, Calvin Bagley's *Hiding from the School Bus* is for you. His journey from a poverty-stricken, illiterate, extreme religious childhood to a life filled with love and business success proves that you should never give up on yourself, regardless of how dark the present may appear. His story inspires us to stay resilient and steadfast and to 'keep the faith.' Thank you, Calvin Bagley, for allowing us into your heart to share the journey of your life, and all its joy, pain, love and faith. We can all learn a lot from you."

—Dr. Patty Ann Tublin, two-time Amazon bestselling author, coach, consultant and speaker

"Calvin Bagley's story is a powerful reminder that our past doesn't define who we become. From a childhood filled with isolation and adversity, Calvin chose resilience and compassion, becoming someone whose warmth, friendliness and outgoing nature make his difficult background nearly impossible to guess. His journey reveals how deeply someone can transform their life, turn pain into kindness, hardship into strength and struggle into connection. Calvin proves the greatest strength lies not in escaping our past, but in reshaping it into something beautiful."

—Ryan Crownholm, entrepreneur and author of *The Hustle Trap: A How-To Guide for Doing Less and Making More with Your Business*

"Calvin Bagley's story offers a brave, unflinching look at childhood trauma—and more importantly, the courageous road to healing. As someone who believes deeply in the power of reclaiming your joy and rewriting the story of your past, I was moved by Calvin's vulnerability and strength. His journey is a reminder that we are not defined by what we've endured, but by how we choose to rise from it."

—Janelle Bruland, author of *Your Way Back to Happy*

"Calvin Bagley flips the script on suffering. He turns trauma into fuel and isolation into impact. His story proves that love—real, raw, earned love—can rewrite your life. This isn't just healing. It's reinvention. It's what happens when you stop managing your past and start creating your future."

—Richie Norton, international bestselling author of *Anti-Time Management* and *The Power of Starting Something Stupid*

"What's most remarkable about Calvin Bagley isn't just the unthinkable childhood trauma he endured, but the man he chose to become. His journey shows you that true courage and freedom lie in facing your wounds, doing the hard work to heal and sharing your truth so others can find light in their own darkness."

—Martha McSally, former United States senator, fighter pilot, keynote speaker, author of *Dare to Fly: Simple Lessons in Never Giving Up*

"There are moments and memories that Calvin Bagley shares in *Hiding from the School Bus* that will make you want to hug him and be there with him to soften the blows. Though he's been through so much, he's remained insightful and sensitive, and learned that not all people will hurt you and that there is good in the world. I'm proud to help in any way to get this story to someone who needs to see what is possible."

—Dr. Don Wood, CEO of Inspired Performance Institute

For more information about Calvin Bagley and *Hiding from the School Bus*, scan the QR code below:

CONTENTS

1. ON THE KNIFE'S EDGE

THE SOUND OF STEEL MEETING WHETSTONE, SLOWLY AND deliberately, is a rhythmic scrape that rises and falls with each circular pass. With the first dramatic thrust of steel onto stone, so begins the holy sacrament of my father sharpening his knife blade.

He sits at the kitchen table, hunched over his tools with the same intensity I imagine blacksmiths once had. His hands, stained with dirt and calloused from labor, move with practiced care. No apron, no theatrics—just a man in a stained white button-down shirt, spitting on a worn sharpening stone as if the act itself held sacred authority. In a 1980s world of dishwashers, microwaves and color TVs—none of which existed in our home —our house was filled with anachronistic artifacts. Chief among them was my father.

As the rhythm quickens, I feel my breathing become ragged and labored. I tamp down my panic, knowing surely that my father will take out his aggression on something—someone—if I interrupt him. I envy the living beings who never see or hear his looming violence. In our home, sounds—or lack thereof—are always warning signs of things to come.

My father performs this ritual countless times throughout my childhood. From his leather belt pouch, worn smooth at the edges from years of use, he produces two items that seem extensions of himself: a pocket knife with a bone handle yellowed by time and a sharpening stone, dark and porous.

When boredom finds him—or perhaps when something darker stirs—he draws them out, gathering saliva in his mouth to spit deliberately onto the stone. The small pool that gathers there glistens momentarily before he begins.

The circular motion is hypnotic, each rotation punctuated by that distinctive sound—part hiss, part song—a metallic lullaby that fills our impossibly small home. Sometimes he pauses to test the edge with his thumb, a gesture so casual it belies the danger. The blade is always keen, ready for whatever purpose he might find for it. I know he is satisfied with his work when the edge is sharp enough to draw blood easily.

My bare toes dig into the cool dirt as I peer up at the row of rabbits, their bodies swaying slightly in the morning breeze. His movements are sudden and perfunctory—grip, slice, release. The creatures dangle from the long pole, their soft brown fur stark against the cloudless sky. Each time his knife flashes in the sunlight, a crimson stream patters onto the earth below, the dust swallowing it hungrily. Drop by drop. Rabbit by rabbit. Tears lodge themselves in my throat where they will stay. I stand frozen like a sentry: impassive, at attention.

The blade dulls by the fourth rabbit, while his movements grow more crude. As he peels back the skin with strained tugs, I notice his hands aren't filling our family's metal pail but a stranger's wooden crate lined with old newspaper. This must be a barter. I should have known—meat is never reserved for us to eat; only strangers are entitled to such a luxury.

I blink hard, my eyes burning but refusing to close. The knife catches the sun again, a brilliant flash that seems almost like a wink between us. His mouth curls slightly at the corner as he moves to the next rabbit. Every so often in the rabbits' final moments, I wonder if we are all here for my father's pleasure.

All of the animals on our five acres serve a specific purpose. The stray cats that live in the barns are generally welcome because my father appreciates their hunting of mice and rodents. Though utility comes first, my mother forms attachments to them anyway, even giving some names. One day, as my father feeds the strays, a frightened kitten hisses and scratches his hand. Obscenities fly from his mouth with such ferocity that I am alarmed that God might hear him; he makes a habit of screaming up at the sky and I am sure someone is listening.

In one swift motion, he seizes the kitten, squeezing its neck as it struggles against his grip. With his free hand, he draws out his freshly sharpened knife. I watch incredulously as my father presses the blade's point against the kitten's skull and slowly pushes inward. My ears abruptly sting with the screech that escapes the kitten's throat. And just as quickly, a murderous silence settles as blood and matter spill.

All there is left to do is obey.

———

The summer my parents met, my mother, Coene, was playing the lead in *My Fair Lady* in the Idaho Falls community theater. Dean, my father, played in the orchestra as first chair violin. That production led to their courtship and marriage on July 8, 1960, when Mom was 20 and Dad was 27.

Their wedding pictures, particularly the pictures of my mom, were beautiful. One particular photo showing the barest hint of décolletage became her peculiar obsession, with my mother simultaneously criticizing and showcasing the photo out loud to no one in particular, epitomizing her contradictory relationship with propriety.

Despite her sustained cruelty over time—or because of it— my mother remains beautiful to this day. As a teenager, I often wondered whether her indifference to our happiness and abject lack of concern for our well-being somehow preserved her beauty like an elixir.

The newlyweds' nomadic existence began in remote British Columbia, where the eldest of my eight siblings, Cynthia, arrived barely a year after their vows. They meandered through California before landing in Salt Lake City. My father's entrepreneurial failures accumulated steadily, with the collapse of a service station partnership marking his descent into eventual permanent unemployment. His subsequent position as a ranch foreman on Ute tribal land relegated us to perpetual outsider status, our fragile tenure mirroring the strained relations between farmers and Indigenous people in the 1970s Uintah Basin.

The Uintah Basin runs from Starvation Reservoir near the town of Duchesne, Utah, to the Colorado border. Its boundaries are the Uinta Mountains, to the north, and the Book Cliffs, to the south.

Our so-called education evolved from homeschooling out of practical necessity into righteous ideology. While Cynthia and the older siblings experienced structured schooling with my mother's earnest if limited oversight, by my era, homeschooling had transformed into religious insulation from worldly corruption.

By the time I was 10, even the pretense of educational materials had vanished from my life. Where I once struggled with untouched workbooks, I learned to accept the absence of knowledge that was my lot. This educational vacuum led me to coin the term no-schooled since homeschooling gained legitimacy through actual structured programs—my experience bearing no resemblance to intentional education. I knew instinctively that my homeschooled peers could see through my veneer of legitimacy if I tried too hard to relate. Even my religious studies consisted of elaborate deceptions, gluing seminary workbook pages together and completing only every tenth assignment, my father's cursory inspection never revealing my shortcuts. Only God would know.

In my younger years, my siblings and I perfected the illusion of studying under my father's negligent eye. We programmed our mannequin poses with the sound of our father's tiller in the garden—its uneven rumbling signaling our freedom to play indoors, books strategically displayed but unopened as we awaited his inevitable water breaks. As much as my father tried to tame the hostile desert earth, the oppressively dry air and unfriendly terrain ensured his thirst was unquenchable and his task forever incomplete.

Our days followed a precise choreography of deception and survival. We ate breakfast at 9 am and dinner at 5 pm—no lunch, no snacks, no late-night indulgences. Just two meals a day. We were hungry all the time.

Morning chores preceded breakfast, after which my father's tiller became our liberating signal. We transformed matchbox cars and homemade basketball hoops into secret entertainment, our ears perpetually attuned to the engine's subtle variations. Should the tilling cease, we instantly materialized as studious children around the kitchen table—a convincing tableau that masked our educational void.

Afternoons almost always gave way to physical labor: hauling rocks, weeding gardens, harvesting crops. Autumn's canning season eliminated even our morning reprieve of indoor freedom. Coerced child labor was as much a hallmark of our childhood as Sunday services.

Every morning began early enough that the sky was still dark, certainly early enough for us to finish before breakfast. The most pressing things for us to finish were the animal chores. My older brothers, Ed and Jeff, would milk the goats, up to 30 at a time. Goats, in my honest opinion, are the worst. I hate goats to this day— we all hate goats. They were always getting themselves into precarious situations that required our immediate attention. They often got their dumb heads stuck in the fence, tried to eat from our garden and made loud, obnoxious bleating noises I can't ever unhear. It was our job to herd them in the sagebrush field next to our home.

There was one time when Jeff was helping Ed herd the goats while also whittling a small piece of wood with a knife. He cut his thigh so deeply it touched the bone. Our parents were not home and we had no way of contacting them, so our older sister, Kate, called our closest neighbor—someone who lived one mile down the road. He and his wife took Jeff to the hospital to get stitches. Our parents later complained about the hospital bill and insisted that a butterfly bandage would have been sufficient mending to close the wound.

My father's occasional errands in town granted rare and unsupervised outdoor adventures, though we remained vigilant for passing vehicles and the dreaded school bus. My mother's warnings that educational authorities might forcibly enroll us if our truancy were discovered terrified me. Later, my fear of school stemmed from an awareness of my profound ignorance. Meeting properly educated homeschooled peers who transitioned successfully to high school only confirmed my recognition of the irreparable gap in my knowledge.

When a tribal member qualified for my father's position with the Ute tribe, they defenestrated him without hesitation. My father then clumsily and inexpertly ventured into the newspaper business. Armed with only the wishful daydreams of becoming a writer, his lack of know-how predictably led to the paper's downfall.

After investors salvaged the remnants, my mother ironically secured employment selling advertising for the revived publication, working there for four decades while my father stalled in his ability to provide for our family.

His final stab at employment, driving a water truck for oil fields, briefly made me aspire to follow in his footsteps. I vividly remember accompanying him when I was four to a drilling platform where a three-fingered worker urged me toward college instead of menial labor. As young as I was, this encounter planted the first seed of doubt about my parents' educational philosophy, suggesting college might offer upward mobility rather than corruption.

———

My parents were stunningly able to appear normal to our church community, primarily because they hid behind their musical talents. My father on violin accompanied my mother's increasingly vibrato-heavy singing. No good performance could go unpunished—each blamed the other for their deteriorating skills, establishing a pattern of mutual recrimination that characterized their relationship. In art as in life, they were eternally devoted to their shared joylessness.

Though my parents outwardly subscribed to the beliefs of The Church of Jesus Christ of Latter-day Saints, which is more commonly known as the Mormon Church or the LDS Church, what they practiced more closely resembled an uninformed extremist approach. Beneath their religious facade and moral turpitude lurked a terrifying capacity for violence. My sister once recounted our mother holding a butcher knife over my oldest brother Ed when he was a baby, while screaming at her daughters about chores. Years later, when the same sister who confronted her about wielding a knife brought up this incident, our mother vehemently denied it. Yet mysteriously, the knife in question disappeared—her disposal of the weapon more damning than any confession.

My parents' extremism is a bit complex in the greater context of LDS tenets. They didn't practice polygamy, which is what fundamentalist Mormons are known for. There was, however, a large amount of overlap between their extreme beliefs and those of polygamists: homeschooling, isolationism, poverty, homesteading, severe distrust and contempt for the government and anti-medical establishment sentiment. Their deep skepticism was exacerbated by events like those that took place at Ruby Ridge. My father was friends with infamous polygamists like the Singer and Swapp families. He once took our family to visit them when I was just a baby. Cynthia insists that he wanted her and another one of my sisters to marry John Singer's sons.

In 1979, John Singer—a Mormon fundamentalist who practiced polygamy and homeschooled his children—was shot dead by police during a raid on his family's compound. My parents were convinced he was killed because he defied the government by homeschooling his children. Nine years later, his son-in-law Addam Swapp believed God had spoken to him—that on the anniversary of John Singer's death, Singer would be resurrected and Christ would return.

At 3 a.m. on January 16, 1988, Swapp and Singer's widow Vickie planted 50 pounds of dynamite inside an LDS chapel in Marion, Utah, detonating it and causing over a million dollars in damage. Within hours of the blast, 150 federal agents surrounded the embattled homestead where six adults and nine children barricaded themselves inside. The family refused all attempts at negotiation, even when officials sent in a fellow fundamentalist to mediate. For thirteen days, the siege continued. In the firefight that eventually broke out, Swapp was wounded. As armored vehicles stormed the compound, he finally surrendered, waving a blood-stained white towel. The revelation had failed—John Singer remained dead and his followers faced prison.

My parents' beliefs were less dramatic, but still different and strange—with isolation from the world marking their descent into á la carte, boutique Mormonesque theology that deluded them into thinking they were holier than all of the church members around us.

We weren't allowed to eat chocolate, listen to modern music, eat pork and beef, wear shorts, or inexplicably, own our own toothbrushes—though lack of dental hygiene was more a product of poverty than anything else. Dental accoutrements were so foreign to us—as were tiny luxuries like candy—that my younger brother Ben and I would eat tiny dollops of toothpaste as if it were the same as eating high-fructose corn syrup. We had quite an exciting Christmas one year when Santa left travel tubes of toothpaste for us in our stockings, never mind that they were one of our only gifts.

Even more confusingly, my parents immiserated our family by choice, forcing a vow of poverty on us as young children who couldn't possibly make a choice like that for ourselves. If we disobeyed them, we would be accused of apostasy and punished accordingly. They were convinced that public schools were corrupting influences over innocent children, encouraging students to be worldly. Neither government nor law enforcement could be trusted.

Collecting taxes was the Original Sin that ought to be made illegal in their eyes. The healthcare system was one large evil conglomerate keeping us reliant on human power. The only reasons we were permitted to go to the hospital were needing stitches or being on the verge of death. My father once lived for three days with a ruptured appendix, untreated. His attempted cure was self-administered enemas of colloidal silver.

What made my dad's version of colloidal silver certifiably insane was that he created it himself. He would take a large battery pack and a pure silver bar, submerge the silver in water and use the battery pack to pass electricity through the silver. The process created electrolysis to the extent that silver would break up into pieces in the water. On a good day, making something considered unregulated and dubious with no safety controls in place is incredibly dangerous. There was no way to know how much silver was in the water. As my dad aged, his skin became almost slate grey from constant misuse over the years.

Black salve is another one of my mother's favorite alternative treatments to this day. It is a topical agent believed to cure illnesses like skin cancer. It is made of extremely toxic ingredients, including bloodroot and zinc chloride. My mother is convinced that if my sister, Kate, had applied the correct amount of black salve to her skin after her cancer diagnosis, she would still be alive today.[1]

My parents were disillusioned and sad that the church supported efforts of funding and administering millions of vaccines around the world. They often voiced disagreement with local church leaders behind closed doors. Dad's predominant opinion was that the Prophet surely hadn't weighed in, therefore the local leadership had gone rogue. I think it was his way of reconciling Christ's true church supporting something as abhorrent as vaccines.

———

Our parents had their worst fights under the cloak of darkness.

As a child, I felt their contempt for one another deep in the marrow of my bones. Awakening to fits of screaming, I'd press my ear to the floor, tracking the escalating arguments below. Their predictable spiral began with hushed intensity, mother's shrill *Deeeeeaaaannn* followed by father's cursing, culminating in physical struggles, slamming doors and shattered mirrors. My siblings gathered for comfort while I, terrified yet transfixed, recognized the intoxicating power of rage flowing through me. Only dawn's arrival dissipated the darkness, revealing my father's hasty departures and the mirror's fractured face—repeatedly broken into ghoulish shards, taped, replaced and broken again—our very own funhouse mirror.

Another violent memory crystallized when I was eight: my parents arguing by the coal pile as my older sister Kate and I watched secretly from the upstairs window in our crowded bedroom. When my mother attempted to escape in her car, my father hurled a massive coal chunk at her windshield.

I could tell by his earnest aim that he meant to strike her, though she barely escaped as the momentary missile crashed behind. The horror of witnessing my father's murderous intent paralyzed me while Kate's scream shattered both the moment and the hairbrush she gripped with all her fright. By morning, their cold détente restored the usual tension.

Our family's isolation in the remoteness of the desert intensified my parents' irrationality. Their religious delusions and increasingly strict rules heightened the tension in our home. My father maintained that children were unformed clay for parents to mold, a belief perhaps challenged only by his children's increasing resistance.

His cavalier attitude toward his own children's psychological safety mixed with his casual violence toward animals created a daily minefield we learned to hopscotch. I don't know that I can ever forgive my father for using his .22 to shoot our sick dog Mitzi while her canine companion Fritz watched in terror. Each violent episode made me wonder if humans might be next.

When I was five, my father suffered a workplace accident that permanently scarred his face and psyche. The truck hatch explosion that fractured his cheekbone marked his permanent retreat away from gainful employment. Later, he justified his inability to provide for the family by claiming that my mother had insatiable material demands, even while church leaders preached about paternal financial responsibilities to his family. She eventually earned more than my father ever had, though it still was meager when it came to covering expenses for such a large family.

Financial instability hung over our childhood like a permanent storm cloud. The idea of losing our house to the IRS or the bank terrified me less than the thought of losing the garden that had become our primary food source. Among the remnants of my father's failures, the ambition of subsistence farming lay as fallow as our land—our broken clan squeezing blood from a stone, fighting pangs of hunger, hemming in our despair.

We lived and labored as big families once did at the turn of the century. It was as if we lived in tenement housing in a big, bustling city during the age of industrialization when child labor was the norm. Our near destitution was a choice, as if my parents took a vow of poverty on behalf of the entire family. The one thing they deemed unforgivable was receiving any government-based welfare.

The glaring exception was the handful of times my mother was willing to accept help from *church* welfare programs; aid sanctioned by the church was somehow less offensive. Both of my parents felt embarrassed that things were so dire that we had to lean on human aid, so it was difficult for them to go to the bishop to ask for help.

On the first Sunday of every month, members of the church participated in what's called the Fast and Testimony Meeting. Members believe that fasting once a month is a practice that brings us closer to God. The fast typically lasts 24 hours, beginning on Saturday and ending on Sunday.

Fasting is usually accompanied by a Fast Offering, a monetary donation meant to represent the amount of money you would have spent on meals during the period of fasting. The funds from Fast Offerings are spent on people in need within the geographic area, at the discretion of the bishop.

The church produces an impressive array of provisions in the Bishop's Storehouses, tiny shops that look like miniature grocery stores. The Relief Society President writes an order that resembles a grocery list and then recipients like my parents can go to the store to fill their orders. Everything in the store was free to us, but the only items my mother was allowed to pick were those that appeared on her food order.

Out of all of the non-perishable items we received, peanut butter was the one staple we never went without. Every meal, without exception, included toast of some kind with a spread.

The fact that Kate was such a gifted bread maker elevated our meals each and every time. My father, ever the pragmatist, often scolded us for eating too much precious peanut butter. His solution to our perceived gluttony was to start rationing out portions every two weeks according to each child's size, but only for the boys. I didn't mind at first, because I considered it a gift to have my very own supply of peanut butter. It didn't take long for me to realize that the portion my dad set aside for me was not at all enough. Both Ben and I ran out of our share before our two weeks of rationing were up.

———

"Hold still."

I winced under the harsh fluorescent lighting of the bathroom. Dad's bumbling and calloused fingers pinched the raw flesh of my hip as he bent my 11-year-old frame awkwardly across his knee, preparing my thin skin for yet another injection of penicillin. My view of the peeling linoleum depressed me almost as much as the fact that my jeans were bunched down around my ankles. I clutched the edge of the porcelain tub in front of me, my knuckles white with strained effort. Through the door left slightly ajar, I heard my mother opening and closing the refrigerator, shuffling across the kitchen. My father was administering yet another home remedy.

"I don't think it's working," I whispered, my voice cracked and raw from three weeks of coughing. "Maybe I need to go to the hospital."

The abrupt snap of the vial's metallic cap echoed through the bathroom. I could tell without looking that Dad was drawing liquid from the small brown bottle labeled "For Veterinary Use Only." The opaque amber glass caught a tiny sliver of light from the window—the same bottle usually nestled between the goat's milk and the margarine we rationed as if it were silky smooth gold.

"Doctors are for emergencies," Dad muttered, flicking the syringe. A droplet of penicillin formed at the needle's tip. "Give this time to kick in."

My lungs compressed and seized with another coughing fit.

Each hack felt like tiny razor blades dragging across my chest. With one more obscenely loud cough, I watched as blood droplets escaped my mouth and splattered onto the peach-colored tub. There it was, my own blood, cast like paint speckles across the tub's surface. I waited for my father's alarm.

He pretended not to notice.

"Deep breath now," he said, the needle hovering over my pallid skin.

I inhaled as deeply as my imperiled lungs would allow, expecting a sharp pinch. Instead, I was met with a violent stab, as if my father harpooned me. The viscous liquid burned beneath my skin, spreading slowly, like molten glass. Internally, I yelped in pain. But I knew better than to expose my weakness by crying out, lest I invite a lecture on fortitude.

"There." Dad half-smiled, then set the empty syringe on the edge of the sink. "Seventh one's the charm."

The room spun slightly. I fixed my jeans to fit me properly— though the hand-me-downs I inherited seldom did.

"Can I have some vitamin C?" I asked, voice quivering.

He looked at me skeptically, then permitted me to go with one nod. I eyed the orange tablets on my mother's bedside table, tucked behind dozens of tinctures—golden seal, lobelia, garlic oil—nothing more than placebos as far as I was concerned. Ben and I shared a liking to some of her homeopathic pills because when we took them, our gnawing hunger lessened a little.

I hungrily snatched up four tablets that quickly dissolved on my tongue, their chalky taste a strange comfort.

I awoke that night with a sudden, sharp gasp. Clutching at my chest, I quickly realized that I could not catch my breath. I panicked, grasping at my sheets while my lungs refused to expand. It felt as if my chest was collapsing in on itself; I feared I might suffocate to death. Ben shifted in his sleep beside me, then gently touched my arm.

"You okay?" he whispered. I couldn't answer, but I kept nodding in the dark anyway.

By some miracle, I made it through the night. I emerged from my room, groggy and sore from all the coughing I must have done in my sleep. My father looked up from his scriptures, taking in my sunken eyes and blue-tinged lips, giving him a visible pause.

"Come with me," he beckoned, already on his way to the car.

The drive to Roosevelt, the town nearest us, stretched on for a small eternity. Each pothole in the road jostled my delicate system, sending sharp jolts to my chest. He explained that the penicillin usually worked. He didn't skip a beat before he layered this observation with rants about how modern medicine creates dependencies in unsuspecting people.

A serious-looking doctor greeted us in our bay at the ER. He drew the curtain back, never once looking up from his clipboard. Once he did, his expression shifted from disaffected to hardly concealed alarm. My father came to his own defense, interrupting the doctor immediately with a tangle of words meant to justify his treatment regimen for me.

"You've been administering...horse penicillin?" The doctor's pen froze.

"Yes sir, I have," Dad replied. His ego still refused to deflate, despite the doctor's incredulous expression. "Usually clears things right up."

I felt the color rise in my cheeks, despite my translucent skin.

"Horse medications are specifically formulated for animals that weigh 1,000 pounds," the doctor replied carefully. "Humans, especially children, are not built for that kind of dosage."

"We're careful with the dosage," my father insisted as I sank lower into the hospital bed. The doctor's eyes met mine for barely a second–long enough for me to recognize a look so forlorn that it took me years to realize it was pity that I saw on his face.

The doctor looked down for a few moments before he continued, "He has advanced pneumonia and needs antibiotics immediately." And with that, he scribbled on his notepad and thrust a prescription at my father. Before he closed the door behind him, he turned toward us one last time. "Do me a favor—stop treating your children with animal medicine. Next time he might not be so lucky."

I don't know if it was my father's pride or willful ignorance, but he continued to rely on his version of self-medicating for the duration of my childhood. Those antiquated medicine bottles continued to jangle from the refrigerator door shelf each time we opened and closed the door.

Later in my life, this upbringing shaped my complex relationship with modern medicine. On one hand, I found myself in awe of what science could accomplish. On the other, I carried an ingrained suspicion—a deep reluctance to accept all medical advice at face value. It's a strange dissonance to live with: marveling at what modern medicine is capable of while simultaneously questioning many of its recommendations. Over time, I've come to believe there's wisdom in both worlds. I now rely on a mix of holistic and conventional approaches, using whichever one serves best in the moment. Healing, I've learned, doesn't have to pick sides.

Three days after my brush with modern medicine, I spent the afternoon slowly breathing fresh air and sunshine in and out of my lungs. I no longer struggled to breathe because of pills in a small orange bottle with a childproof cap, prescribed by strangers who saved people's lives.

For the moment, I could breathe easier.

2. THE UGLY SPLENDOR OF JUNIPER TREES

KATE FOLDED HER LEGS BENEATH HER ON THE THREADBARE RUG, careful to remain modest. At seventeen, she was ten years older than me, so it was her job to set a Christ-like example. My eyes darted to chase the dust motes swirling around her in the slanted rays of the sun. In this light, her brown hair turned to golden honey. She trained her gaze to never lose mine, those blue eyes anchoring me to the floor. Her softness smoothed the edges of my parents' constant screaming. I could never quite steel myself for the reverberations of slammed doors.

My small fingers traced the letters on the pages of my phonics book. I couldn't stop fidgeting with it, tearing away at the binding already cracked from dedication. I mimicked how I saw my older siblings read from the scriptures, crafting sounds with my mouth, hoping I could guess my way into saying the correct words.

"Mom says you're teaching me to read!" I blurted out, eagerly awaiting our first lesson at that very moment. Kate smiled wryly at me, nodding to herself while thumbing through my book.

In our living room, the alphabet stretched across the top of the wall like a colorful banner of prayer flags. In my eager mind,

I had already started to commit to memory all of the letters I saw in order, except I couldn't determine if the alphabet began with ABC or ZYX. This confusion led me to the accidental accomplishment of memorizing the entire alphabet backward, something I found more than a little tricky to unlearn. This became a quirky party trick I can still perform to this day.

Kate, with her fair complexion, blue eyes and light-brown wavy hair, was the fourth child in our family. Born under the mountain-ringed skies of Salt Lake City, she was always the peacemaker in our chaotic household. She was a gentle soul who recoiled from the frequent arguments that erupted among siblings, often aftershocks we felt from our parents' explosive fights. Her unwavering faith in scripture and devotion to the gospel of Christ soothed her, providing the kind of solace I aspired to achieve.

When I pleaded with my mother about learning to read, she nodded thoughtfully, saying, "Yes, you're about old enough now," before officially assigning Kate as my teacher. My mother often outsourced her maternal duties to my older sisters: teaching us to read, comforting us when we were sad and protecting us from harm. Kate had already guided Jeff through the phonics reading course—a challenging experience, as the two butted heads like stubborn mountain rams. Kate patiently took both Jeff and me through the course. I flourished quickly, while Jeff continued to struggle.

When my three older sisters suddenly departed home, Kate ascended to the position of the eldest remaining child. She blossomed in this role, becoming an exceptional bread maker whose creations filled the house with mouth-watering aromas. In some ways, her elevated role lulled me into a false sense of security, if only for moments at a time. She was a talented cook who could transform simple ingredients into delicious meals. Most days, that was enough to distract me from reality.

Kate took her responsibility as the eldest at home seriously, often patrolling the house with a wooden spoon tucked into her back pocket—a symbol of authority meant to keep her younger brothers in line. Jeff, too strong-willed and physically imposing to be controlled, once stole and snapped her wooden spoon in defiance.

She maintained gentle but firm authority over Ben and me. Unlike our parents, Kate did not need to dominate us physically or verbally to make a lasting impact. We were satisfied with her gentle discipline as a needed reprieve from the norm.

I watched with intense fascination as a scorpion scuttled across fissures in the ground slightly ahead of me, countless limbs tip-toeing around spent shell casings from unknown sources—signs of past danger, if nothing else. Its pincers snapped at the dry air with ferocious speed. I held my breath, crouching low in time to see its tail arc violently. I wanted desperately to call my brother over to see this marvel, but he was too far away to risk vulnerability to such a dangerous arachnid. I remained unassailable in my silence and distance, allowing echoes of my brother's laughter to fill the sprawling meadow behind me.

As a child, I revered the legend of the scorpion falling on its own sword, stinging itself when cornered by fire. I admired how it chose death on its terms, like a kamikaze fighter pilot or a samurai—one final act of defiant control.

It would be years before cursory research disabused me of this notion. Scorpions, it turns out, are immune to their own venom—no suicidal instincts exist in their arsenal. The myth I held in my childhood crumbled, leaving only the sting of truth.

If only I had an antidote for the poison coursing through my veins all these years.

There was so much life teeming in the seemingly barren land around us, as if by miracle. Gnarled, disfigured and unsettling juniper trees scarred the sage meadows, appearing more like bleached bones jutting from the cracked earth, slowly ossifying under the sun's rays. In the distance, I can still hear the door open and close, followed by our mother yelling for us to come inside. However far away we were, we could discern her voice calling for us with impatience and sometimes contempt.

There were so many unstructured hours that stretched in front of us each day, taunting us with boredom, labor and ever-present hunger. We knew well that whatever meal my sister prepared there wouldn't be enough food and we would be left wholly unsatisfied. Playing outside was more than an escape. We took our parents' doctrine of "out of sight, out of mind" literally.

Ben and I exercised our creativity in finding all the ways we could disappear enough to avoid the punishment of a perpetually disappointed mother. Worse than her disapproval, we would be put to work: washing dishes, cleaning, folding or re-folding towels if our work did not pass muster. She even had us rub her feet as if in a spa, which I sometimes had to do for hours at a time.

One day, as I sat on the makeshift swing we hung by rusted chains, my weight tugging on the tenuous branch of a juniper tree. With abandon, I climbed as high as I could, furiously pumping my feet as the wind rushed at my face. Ben scaled the branches above me, making his way to the top of the tree. On a strong impulse, I jumped off the swing, unburdening the weakened branch. It sprang upward, trapping Ben's foot between it and the trunk.

Despite my desperate efforts, his foot remained wedged firmly in the wooden vice. Ben was only six years old to my eight, becoming increasingly terrified by the second. I breathlessly promised to fetch help and sprinted toward home, leaping over sagebrush like a young antelope. The landscape ahead blurred as I raced toward safety, avoiding cacti hidden among the scattered, banded rocks.

I found Kate absorbed in a book, her peaceful reverie immediately abandoned when she registered my panicked expression. Without hesitation, she raced alongside me across the rugged terrain. Upon reaching Ben, who was clutching the tree with eyes squeezed shut, softly singing "I Am a Child of God" through his tears to ward off imagined mountain lions, Kate quickly assessed the situation. With determined strength, she pulled down on the immovable branch, magically releasing Ben's foot. She held his head to her chest and repeated softly, "You are safe now."

She rescued Ben, as no one else could.

———

The rock formations surrounding our land were an imperfect arena, but I felt they were the most trustworthy keepers of our family's secrets. The rocks still display a remarkable range of colors—deep reds, oranges, pinks, whites and yellows. This enviable color palette showcases nature's grandeur, further reminding me of the natural beauty that always felt inaccessible to me, an undeserving spectator.

I imagined heavenly hosts welcoming me one day—if only I could become worthy.

The land below was a hostile and reluctant witness to the unfolding of my dysfunctional childhood. I could taste the dust in my mouth the moment I stepped outside. I never grew bold enough to forget the High Desert of the Uintah Basin had ultimate power over me, not unlike my parents. At times, I'd lose myself admiring the cathedral of shale, limestone and sediment above me, though I had a healthy enough fear to keep a respectful distance.

Our proximity to our Ute tribe neighbors exaggerated historical tensions over land, water rights and jurisdictional matters. Conflict marred my inner and outer worlds as tensions ratcheted up between Utes and farmers.

Wildfires burned through trees and brush periodically, always harbingers for difficult things to come. I was spellbound by the way the trees on each rockface looked after a fire. Their trunks and branches were laid bare, charred by the flames. They resembled electrocuted stick figures who'd stuck their long, thin twig fingers into a light socket. I was inspired by the fact that those same trees stood for so long after they'd been burned, memorializing their own lives, refusing to crumble into ash.

Irrigation canals threaded through the area, collecting and diverting water at varying volumes and speeds. Shocks of neon green alfalfa fields were bright patches of land dotting the dusty, monochromatic desert. Water pumped freely into those fields, alfalfa being the single most prominent crop grown by local farmers who then created bales of hay to feed their livestock.

Water rights were a divisive topic among all residents, Utes and farmers in equal measure. We named the arbiter who presided over our water the "Ditch Rider." As a child, I envied how easily the Ditch Rider could give and take on a whim, the rest of us serving at his pleasure.

I preferred racing our tiny homemade boats in the canals over hauling enormous rocks like our dad expected us to every day. We could never tell before we started work for the day whether he would direct us to build up embankments by stacking the rocks or to clear patches of land for him to garden. Our days unfolded always—always—according to the dictates of the most unpredictable men in my life: my father and the Ditch Rider.

Our land was tempestuous—mercurial, even. I recognized how readily our surroundings oscillated between revealing their gifts and withholding our nourishment. Surveying the horizon as I often did, my eyes narrowed instantly to fields strewn with oil rigs, their harsh silhouettes like pterodactyl skeletons against the sky. We lived near a town that time seemed to have forgotten: Vernal, in northeastern Utah. Vernal is part of the Uintah Basin, with the Uintah Mountains to the north. It is most famous for its dinosaur bones. The endless massive rock structures reflect the history of Vernal's dinosaur fossil fame: the popular Dinosaur Rock Quarry. What were once barely hidden bones suddenly offered a gargantuan surprise to the archaeologists, scientists and geologists who studied here mere decades ago.

Those same fossils were not just well-preserved secrets of the past come to light; they held the promise of large stores of oil. And as quickly as the prized oil reserves were discovered, inquiring minds realized that the liquid was almost exclusively trapped in shale; the land wouldn't easily surrender its oil until forced to do so through fracking.

I couldn't help but think of my father's stubborn agricultural pursuits with his loyal rototiller, trying and failing to force the unyielding earth beneath us to bend to his will—sustenance be damned.

I felt humbled the most by my place at the foot of the mountains. I knew the power of my parents was omnipresent, somehow seeming bigger and more imposing than the rocks that surrounded me. Our family was part of this land, occasional observers of God's glory as we fulfilled our earthly duties. It was not until I first left this place that I felt the absence of an immense pressure resting on my shoulders. As I traveled further away in distance and time—out of sight, out of mind—the burden I thought was once removed became an invisible tonnage of repressed memories always hovering over me. Flashbacks of my childhood were nothing more than anvils over my head.

I toiled like Sisyphus, continuing to roll his boulder up the mountain only to be crushed by its oppressive weight the harder he tried to fight gravity. Me, with my crushing memories; my father, with his obstinacy and refusal to be wrong.

Towering monoliths and improbably stacked rocks made me feel as if I were an astronaut exploring distant planets. My intrusive thoughts often dared me to peek over the steep sides of mesas and buttes, jutting massifs nudging me to jump without a plan. I found comfort in knowing that the narrow and twisting passages of the canyons below came to be throughout hundreds of thousands of years of erosion, their surfaces battered and worn away by water and wind. I prayed for God to give me the patience of Job to wait my turn; I wanted Him to sculpt and mold me into a thing of beauty, too, however long it might take.

———

When I was three years old, my primary teacher at church once told us we should enjoy all of God's beautiful creations like the trees and the birds. I loved nature and all of its mysteries, so I sang and sang to show my devotion.

One Sunday at home after church, I decided that I was going to go for a walk to greet all of God's beautiful creations. No one —not my parents, not my older siblings—noticed that I had wandered off by myself down the winding country road. I walked along the side of the road, outpaced only by the jackrabbits popping up nearby. Time meant nothing to me, so I kept walking and giving thanks to God with my songs.

Hours passed before a man in a truck saw me doddering down the road, laughing to myself while pointing at birds and trees. He was alarmed; there wasn't a house or adult in sight. The Good Samaritan stopped and asked me, "What are you doing out here by yourself, son?" I told him about my Primary teacher's lesson on celebrating all of God's beautiful creatures. He frowned in thought, then quickly put me in his truck. He drove by the closest homes he knew of, slowing down to help me search for my family. When we finally found my house, it was immediately clear that no one knew I was missing. The man handed me to my parents cautiously, stepping back to distance himself. "Ok, I'll be on my way then," he said, vanishing without a single word more.

I don't remember them thanking him.

———

My family's trailer—my first home—was parked adjacent to what I later learned is Skinwalker Ranch. Legend has it that the ranch and its adjoining lands permeate with paranormal activity. In 1789, a treaty was broken between the Ute and Navajo tribes. When the U.S. government established the Northern Ute Reservation by presidential decree in 1860, native peoples did not take too kindly to these encroaching forces. Later that year, the Utes officially joined American troops in a campaign against the Navajo, thereby inviting the Navajo's Skinwalker Curse.[2]

In the years since, whispers of strange noises and unidentified aircraft hovering overhead persist. Outside of hyperspectral imaging technology, the only evidence I had of the Skinwalker were the raised hairs on my arms whenever I breached an invisible boundary. Or perhaps the intermittent occasions of a queasy stomach and temporary spells of dizziness.

As a boy, I felt that my life—dangling at the end of a haunted dirt road—might be swallowed whole.

Eventually, there would come a time when the horror of my daily life eclipsed that of native lore.

Skinwalkers were the least of my worries.

———

"Coyote was sitting, watching Bear. He wanted to kill her. He was sneaking around. A little bird was there and saw him. The bird kept saying, 'Coyote is moving, Coyote is moving.' When he said that, Coyote got angry and threw a rock at him and broke his leg. Then Coyote was sorry and said, 'Oh, I broke my friend's leg.' He got some grass and tied it around the leg and fixed it. Then he killed Bear and took the claws. He made a necklace for the bird. That is why the bird has black around his neck." [3]

I was never comfortable with how much death was around us. So the surprising joy my family expressed collectively at finding a pair of bluebirds to call our own disarmed me, if only to give me small satisfaction with their unusual affection for living things. Every year those same bluebirds would come back and rest in the eaves of our house. They mate for life, so we knew our visitors well—the pride of our family. We understood never to interfere with such a treasure, though we would often shoot recklessly at barn swallows and magpies. Those undesirable birds were universally considered worthy of disgust and disdain, giving me tacit permission to aim at them for target practice.

My brothers and I made our own slingshots—what we called "wrist rockets." Our invention had a steadying force to it, more powerful than a simple slingshot because of the force you could exert. Though we played well enough together, I often bore the brunt of my older siblings' teasing. Ben would have as well—he and I were close enough in age—but he was "Gentle Ben." I was an awkward, verbose chatterbox who held my siblings hostage just to have a captive audience. Whenever we played with our wrist rockets, we spent most of the time gathering pebbles from the dusty ground. Even I proved to be useful in our quest to find the best ammo.

When all love was unrequited in my limited experience of the world, I was willing to take attention in its place.

More than anything, I wanted to impress my older brothers.

One sleepy afternoon, I spotted a beautiful blue bird perched on the fence post. Though I was alone, I knew if I hit the bird squarely, I would have bragging rights for weeks to come. I steadied my feet and took my aim. I let go of the sling, willing my pebble to meet its mark. And just as quickly as I had dismissed my shot as a loss, the weightless bird flew up into the arc of my missile. It flew into my pebble as surely as if I had hit it directly. No living thing was there as a witness.

My first reaction was a yelp of joy and pride. My brothers couldn't possibly make fun of me when they saw what an incredible shot I was. But as quickly as I beamed, a wave of shock and remorse washed over me when the reality of what I'd done hit me. In my eagerness to please, had I inadvertently killed one of our family's bluebirds?

I hesitated as I ambled forward, hoping that the movement I sensed just up ahead was not what I feared it might be. When I came upon my victim, I saw its wings flapping haplessly on the ground—one of our beloved bluebirds wounded at my hand. In that moment, I instinctively secured my misadventure as a secret to be filed away in the deep recesses of my mind.

There was no reality in which I could tell my siblings or my parents that I injured one-half of our prized bluebird couple and receive anything less than a violent reaction. I felt so wicked that I could bring pain upon something so innocent. My heart became laden with shame and my shoulders slumped beneath the weight of my sin. I never wanted to wield power the way my father did. But I was no different than he. At that moment, I began to observe the Bagley family tradition of secret-keeping all on my own.

With moist eyes and a quivering bottom lip, I tracked the bluebird limping around our yard. I prayed obsessively to God to let the bird live—to spare its suffering. To my horror, one of the barn cats stalked behind me; it struck to kill, then ate the bird. A plume of cerulean feathers was instantly strewn around our yard as I looked on helplessly, speculating who was now predator and who was prey. My tormented heart and anxious mind caused a sensation I had never felt before:

I was scared of myself.

I was, in fact, capable of the same violence I resented in my parents.

At that very moment, the familiar sputter of a car engine punctured the sound barrier of silence in the isolated countryside. I dropped the evidence of my depravity and turned to walk slowly toward our house. I would bury this secret and carry it with me to my grave.

My mother looked almost ghostly in the pale wash of the moonlight. She hummed quietly, her fingers drumming the steering wheel as she leaned forward to squint through the windshield. As a child, I often closed my eyes while driving this stretch of road at night, whether I was tired or not. The velvety curtain of darkness surrounding us hung heavily enough to scare me with its dangerous stillness.

I watched my mother intently as I entertained myself singing my favorite songs. Wilma, my church Primary teacher, rode along with us in the passenger seat. The three of us—Wilma, mom and I—took turns singing one of our favorite Primary songs, *Sing Your Way Home*. I cheerfully sang the verse with all the verve and gusto I could generate as a child:

Sing your way home at the close of the day.
Sing your way home; drive the shadows away.
Smile ev'ry mile, for wherever you roam
It will brighten your road, it will lighten your load
If you—

CRASH.

An oncoming car turned on its brights, a force so strong I had to squint to make out what was in front of us. The light revealed an enormous horse standing in the middle of the pothole-riddled road with no sense of urgency or fright, as if he had nowhere to be but there, with us.

A split second before we hit the horse, he came into view in the jaundiced glow of our old Volkswagen Rabbit's clouded headlights. In that tenth of a second, I saw his body was turned away from us with his elegant neck craning his head toward the approaching lights.

A swish of his tail.

A flash of dark coals smoldering like embers meeting my

eyes–a hideous and final blow. Metal crumpled. Glass shattered. The air paused.

Moments later, my eyes flickered open. The blur before me was perhaps red numbers blinking on the dashboard or blood from any one of our car's passengers. Something warm and wet trickled down my cheek—it tickled, but not in the way I liked. My mother lurched at us in the dark, her fingers spreading blood across the vinyl seats as she groped for our hands. Her voice trembled with each name she called out. She shoved open her car door, shouting instructions at me with urgency.

"Keep pushing the horn. Don't stop laying on the horn."

Horrified but happy to have a task to complete, my eyes followed our mother stumbling around the mangled grill of the car to the passenger seat. She leaned into the space once occupied by its glass window, stopping short with a quiet gasp. There in the passenger seat lay someone—something—where Ms. Wilma once sat. In her place was a grotesque display of tissue, organs and skeletal remains exploded on the seat, unrecognizable as someone I knew, as someone at all.

My throat tightened.

"Don't look at Wilma," our mother whispered, her voice becoming a low moan. "She's not with us anymore."

I pressed my palm firmly at the horn's center. An excruciating blare traveled across empty fields of sage brush echoing through the surrounding tribal land. The car moved unexpectedly, causing my head to throb.

My mother had scooped up Ben, cradling his limp body to her chest. She continuously murmured words as if in solemn prayer, praying for our deliverance. She turned the key to start the engine, the car creeped forward once again. The car moved so slowly that I thought we might never reach help. Two more miles to Whiterocks where I could rest my aching hand that still pressed the horn unceasingly.

Finally, lights flickered on at the Arrowches's house as our car approached. The Arrowches family was prominent in our community, always willing to help their neighbors. Mrs. Arrowches ran out to us in her bathrobe with a squawking radio already in her hand. She must have seen us approaching, must have known we were all mangled in some way. She had medical training, a fact I now know makes her an angel in such unimaginable darkness.

By this point, my vision and hearing began to fade in and out as my consciousness waned. I could make out her voice radioing for help.

"Multiple victims...horse struck by vehicle...minors in the back...one fatality."

Mr. Arrowches led us into their living room. It smelled of sage. He grabbed a kitchen towel to press against the gash in my older sister Belinda's forehead. Scarlet flowers bloomed through the thin white fabric.

In the living room, a smoky mirror hung crooked on wood-paneled walls. A strange face stared back at me, dark rivulets traced paths down my cheeks, blood dripping from my chin onto my hand-me-down flannel shirt. The gash across my forehead gaped like a small cavern. I brushed one, then two fingers over the wound, removing them as soon as they became slick with blood. Only then did the pain arrive, mean, hot and sharp.

Sirens suddenly filled the silent living room.

Once we made it to the hospital, a nurse treated my wounds quickly, her gentle hands tilting my chin upward without causing more pain. "Hold still now," she cooed, tweezers poised to remove the glass embedded in my skin. The ping of tiny glass shards hitting the metal tray startled me each time.

Belinda whimpered in the bed next to mine, trying not to resist as a nurse probed her wound with antiseptic ointment.

My beloved Ben, whose death I assumed was nigh, peaked through heavy eyelids crying, "It hurts to open my eyes, Mom." His eyes were now covered in butterfly bandages. "You are lucky this little one did not lose his sight," the doctor's words floated distantly above my head.

My little sister Uvene had no such luck.

My baby sister, special since birth, was hooked up to a venti-lator that wheezed rhythmically in the crib she occupied at the tiny rural hospital. Her chest hardly rose or fell with each artifi-cial breath. Uvene was special because God made her perfect as she was, our one sibling born with Down syndrome.

The doctors entrusted with her care spoke in hushed tones using words like "critical condition," "uncertain outcome" and "might not last through the night." The head trauma she experi-enced in the accident had damaged her brain development so that she would forever think and operate as a three-year-old.

The next morning, our church's branch president drove me home from my stay at the hospital. I stared down at the worn floorboards, my headache ever present, only slightly aware of the trees and fields that blurred past us through the window. Instinctively, I sat upright as we approached the bend where I saw it in the harsh clarity of daylight: a morass of deep red stained the road, already tinged brown at its edges.

For the next few weeks, our church members delivered casseroles, green and red Jello molds and desserts to our doorstep—an immovable feast. Our refrigerator was so stuffed it could barely contain it all, but the platters of chocolate chip cookies and brownies went straight to the trash. Our parents believed eating chocolate was a sin. But my stomach knotted whenever I opened the refrigerator door. I was in so much discomfort and pain that the idea of eating a full meal nauseated me to my core.

In my dreams, I could hear Wilma's empty rocking chair sway on her rickety porch, wooden boards groaning under the weight of her absence. She lived miles away, yet somehow close by—a tender mercy—her being one of the few neighbors we had.

I loved Wilma. But more importantly, I *believed* she loved me too.

3. CHOOSING A WILLOW

His COMMANDMENT CAME DOWN WITH A THUNDEROUS ROAR:

"Choose a willow," he bellowed.

Blood and sweat mingled on my face as Ben and I wrestled in the makeshift garden. Dirt and dust clung to our moist skin with every thud of our bodies on the earth, each of us at one time the victor. We seldom fought, yet we proved to be good sparring partners.

I stole one last jab, stumbling to meet empty space before me. As if on cue, our father's shadow sliced the noon sunlight; his presence seemed to discipline the daylight itself. His voice cut through our grunts.

"And peel the bark. You know how," he snarled.

Those words froze my insides and halted my breathing. That instruction began a ritual of terror we knew too well. With each command, he demanded we be complicit in our own torture.

The first time I heard it—that whistle cutting through air—my muscles tensed before my mind could process. The fear and anticipation of the pain stung almost worse than the lashing itself. I envied my brother, Jeff, who defied my father with his laughter. It didn't matter how hard he hit Jeff with a two-by-four, my brother would laugh in his face. But I was unable to find humor in any of this.

Unlike the dull thud of the two-by-four or the crack of the paddle, the willow trilled discordantly. The speed with which it mars skin required all of my attention, as if concentrating would help me manage the pain. In an instant, welts appeared on my supple skin, all raised and rapidly crimson; I swore I could see blood pulse beneath them. I felt myself disassociate for seconds then minutes at a time, imagining a crack in the firmament where a protective God reached down to disarm my father, setting us free. Maybe forever.

In the still moments before his lashings began, I wistfully thought of the words from *Doctrine and Covenants 11:3-4*:

"Behold, the field is white already to harvest; therefore, whoso desireth to reap let him thrust in his sickle with his might, and reap while the day lasts, that he may treasure up for his soul everlasting salvation in the kingdom of God. Yea, whosoever will thrust in his sickle and reap, the same is called of God."

I wondered if this was me, reaping what I had sown. God's will be done, I pleaded.

Ben was my younger brother, the best-behaved and most beloved by our parents. The fact that our fighting was so severe that our father accepted Ben played a part at all made me feel crushing guilt.

Ben and I trudged to the ditch, our heads hanging low and our boots sinking into the mud. The water flowed silently past rows of willow thickets bent prostrate like worshippers at the altar—or mourners at a funeral. Our pocket knives dangled from our belts, reminding us of our ostensible survival skills.

I wondered if today I might die.

The willows towered over us along the ditch bank, their slender reeds swaying slightly as if choreographed for this very moment. I knew not to be seduced by their beauty—willows were nature's whips waiting to be harvested by a knowing hand. We ran our fingers along different reeds, testing their rigidity or flexibility. Thick willows bruised deep, leaving purple marks that ached when you sat. Thin ones left fiery red welts that lingered for weeks, raging when fabric brushed against them. Medium willows were the ideal, we'd learned, through the brutal process of deduction.

I cut a reed close to the ground, struggling to accept what had already begun to unfold. Its bark peeled away in long, wet strips that curled around my fingers like shed snakeskin. The tender wood beneath was smooth and cream-colored. We peeled our willows slowly, methodically, lingering in our final moments before punishment.

The balsam smell of exposed willows suspended my disbelief that evil lurked there. Perhaps these were willows in their prime, a prelude to the sting we'd soon feel elsewhere, everywhere.

Ben had never faced the willow switch before. His eyes flashed with momentary courage as he gripped his freshly disrobed willow and fantasized of fighting back. "What if you hit him first, then I try?"

I shook my head, already capitulating to the enormous letdown of similar rhetorical encounters. "It'll only sting for a second," I lied, hoping to shield him from the matter at hand. Just the stuff of dreams. We were seven and nine, trembling with fear, knowing the price of defiance was far more than we could afford.

We stood at the garden's edge as our father approached first with the spent tiller. The machine growled and spat dirt clods around his ankles. The corral fences pinned us in, reminding me almost too late to watch for discarded barbed wire on the ground around us.

The air smelled of gasoline and freshly turned earth. When silence fell, our father spoke with unmistakable clarity:

"You two face each other. Now hit each other with your willows."

Horror crept up my spine with agonizing certainty. Neither of us ever wanted to harm the other. The memory of our fight had long since evaporated, replaced by mutual fear and unrealized bravery. The willow switches hung limply in our hands, already heavy with consequence, their tiny branches splayed across the dirt, like a toddler's fingers tracing letters in the sand.

"*Do it, Goddamnit!*" he commanded.

One tear unwittingly escaped my eye. Neither of us could move. Our father stared for a moment, then abruptly demanded we drop our willows. He had only his point to prove, wherein our psychological torment was simply collateral damage.

He then proudly bloviated with a lecture on discipline and respect. As I suppressed my tears, I felt the hate crystallize permanently in my chest. He fed off of our fear, satiated only by his self-righteous indignation.

After whipping sessions, I'd lock myself in the bathroom, examining the welts on my skin with an obscene pride. *Look at what I can endure,* I'd think to myself. I'd contort myself to view every single one of the markings I felt before they raised my skin.

Meanwhile, a constellation of pain mapped itself across my limbs, my disobedience made manifest.

The belt left bruises that faded. The paddle numbed before it hurt. But the willow—the willow's lashings lingered, each snap a reminder that refused to fade over a week's time.

Every brush of clothing against my hot skin was a silent accusation.

———

At 15 years old, I once forgot myself entirely.

My mother and I were arguing about school. There was a family in LaPoint that homeschooled their children. They had 10 children, all under the tutelage of their mother. Once each child grew to be of high school age, their parents allowed them to attend a year or two of school. I wanted to go to school so badly it ached to think of what I was missing, of all the things I would never know. I felt overcome with anger and resentment.

"Your homeschool is a total sham," I hissed. "You withheld a real education from me and Ben and we'll never get that back."

My mother continued to ignore me, expressionless.

I felt the ire deep within me climb like ivy up my throat, strangling my fear, voicing only pain. "We are stupid and couldn't even go to school if we wanted to. We know nothing."

This piqued her interest and flamed the fire. "It's your own fault for neglecting your studies. You have no one to blame but yourself." She thrust this as a final shiv in my side, one that should have stopped me cold.

It didn't.

She turned to walk away from me, assuming she had cast the final stone. "You bitch," I spat, mimicking the words I had so often heard my father say to her in disgust. In an instant, she swiveled around, her eyes widening with shock and alarm. She quickly narrowed her gaze to a sadistic glint. At once, her palm cracked against my cheek like a thunderstrike. She seized my wrists with supernatural strength—demons seemed to fortify her movements. I knew my father's physicality was superior to hers, always. She took in a constant stream of verbal abuse from him, often to staggering degrees. But that was not so with me. She overpowered me with hardly any effort at all, aside from that which was required to summon her hellish reinforcements. I winced as her eyes burned black holes into mine, her voice rising to an unholy pitch.

"Do you want me to kill *you*—then kill *myself*?!" she screamed, peering right through me.

The scream peeled paint from walls and shook the panes of our Depression-era glass windows. I bargained with the devil as I collapsed into sobs, begging for forgiveness while her grip loosely held me together. It was then I understood for the first time who had brought me into this world and who could take me out of it—my mother was the true danger in our household. If we were meant to be sealed together as a family for eternity, as we were taught, then I would sew my mouth shut forever.

Maybe I didn't want to be sealed to this family, like an eternal prison sentence. But, for now, one more truth I could swallow, one more vow of silence.

Despite the terror my father inspired by his violent hand, my mother was the parent I feared more. Her brand of slow, methodical emotional manipulation caught me unaware more times than not. She took her time to sow seeds of doubt in her children's hearts, knowing we would question our worth before her and the Lord. Deep grooves have formed in my brain for every memory cemented there, evidence I was not loved, not lovable.

Three days after I was born, my parents drove me home from the hospital to Willow Creek on a 40-mile stretch of side roads carved out near oil fields. The latter part of the journey required driving 20 additional miles on a bumpy dirt road until we reached our trailer. My six older siblings had stayed there by themselves the few days my parents were away.

Cynthia was about to turn 14, the oldest of my siblings. She was the one responsible for keeping our home and watching her younger siblings *in loco parentis*. When my siblings saw the car pull up, they gathered eagerly to see the new addition to the Bagley family. Our mother got out of the car, then immediately handed me over to Cynthia.

"Happy birthday," she said. "This one is yours." And with that, she turned and walked into the trailer.

Cynthia knew before the rest of my siblings that my mother was not joking. She took care of me full-time, doing everything that a mother would do, except feed me—but not without attempting to. On one occasion, my sister felt so consumed by her motherly duties that she tried to breastfeed me. She couldn't, of course, but the thought was what counted. Cynthia was practically a child herself in an impossible situation, strapped with all of the responsibilities of a grown woman—responsibilities that my mother herself wasn't taking on. The only time my mother parented me was when it was time for me to eat.

As the seventh child, I was so forgotten by my mother that she didn't even bother to check my birth certificate when it arrived. If she had, she would've noticed that my legal name was mistakenly listed as "Alvin" instead of "Calvin"—a fact I discovered on my own as a pre-teen.

Eventually, I had to have it legally changed so that my birth certificate matched the name I'd always believed was mine.

I once read about a pre-Darwinian concept known as "maternal impression."[4] This is an antiquated notion that was once widely accepted as fact: the belief that a pregnant woman imprints her biggest fears, loudest thoughts, and biggest moments onto the infant in her womb. I wonder, then, if my mother was at one point in my tiny life the spiritual inscription machine she aspired to be—she was nothing if not a hopeful conspiracist. She and my father viewed their brood of children as a means to an end; that is, we were their insurance for The End Times, their contribution to population growth, a built-in workforce, the ultimate legacy, their ticket to eternal perpetuity sealed to as many souls in the afterlife as possible. We were, in sum, the means rather than an end in and of ourselves.

————

Sitting on Cynthia's lap at the piano is the safest place in the world to me. My favorite thing to do is rest my small hands over hers as she plays songs, for our ears only. I keep my hands still, even when her long fingers tickle mine at every chord change. Melodies lift up her gentle laugh on this cold December afternoon. I breathe in the scent of her hair like strawberries. For now, I am happy.

"Again!" I say, her three-year-old maestro.

My head jerks suddenly as the trailer door slams open. I

shiver when the freezing air rushes in uninvited. My father's silhouette takes up the entire door frame, blocking the way in or out.

"That's *enough*." His gruff voice is off key.

Cynthia hugs me against her, arms tightening around me. "We were just practicing…"

"Stop acting like you're his mother. He already has one." With one command, he disbands our joy, wrenching me from Cynthia's embrace. But before he does, I feel her heart skid in her chest, recklessly beating against my own chest. I grasp at her wool sweater tugging in vain.

"Dean, please," my mother calls out weakly from the kitchen. It is too late; the piano bench scrapes against linoleum as Cynthia stands to reach toward me one last time. I can tell that she means it.

My father yanks me from Cynthia and tosses me to my mother.

"Cynthia, sit down." He points to the floor. "You will not touch him again. Not ever. You will not respond to him when he cries. You are *not* his mother."

Before I understand why, tears stream down my cheeks. Cynthia's face blurs through my veil of tears, her own eyes moist, her cheeks glistening. The harder my mother grips me, the more I thrash against her, my throat starting to become sore from screaming. It's no use; my protests fall on deaf ears.

It feels like I'm drowning—if I open my mouth to scream, I will only swallow water that suffocates me from the inside. The air is thick with my silence.

Cynthia's eyes never leave mine. In that moment, her forlorn but loving gaze imprints on me the way a mother's should. I know now we are bonded together forever, no matter what or who tries to separate us. She is who protects my heart.

Three days later, I discover rage.

I find my older brother Ed's bug collection covered in a thin layer of dust, resting on the shelf he built himself. I hungrily eye the rows of pinned insects he's organized, fastidious in his collection and presentation. These are the opal and onyx insects he's gathered from the five acres surrounding our new Farm Creek house. I waste no time crushing each delicate wing with sadistic relish. I don't bother pulling out the pins. I don't stop ripping and discarding until microscopic parts remain.

Our father's favorite kitchen timer—and preferred projectile to throw at the wall—starts to trill. I snap out of my hazy ire in time to make my escape.

When Ed discovers the remnants of his bug collection, he shouts and sobs uncontrollably. Dad charges up the creaking stairs, ready to punish with a humiliating naked-butt, over-the-knee spanking. I stand in the hallway amid the wreckage I've caused, unrepentant. The rage subsides, but I don't feel better. Watching Ed unable to console himself, I feel only shame and guilt.

Later that night, I wander over to the piano. Somehow, I'd forgotten the dent where my forehead connected with the polished wood before. I trace my fingers over the wood, measuring its length. I slam my head forward.

The pain is white-hot and intoxicating. It drowns the sound of Ed's anguish, the thoughts that chase me from contentment. Blood creeps its way, warm and steady, down my temple. I press my palm against this new dent I've made, my proof of life.

Here, I have permission to exist.

———

I could not wait to turn eight years old. This birthday was a significant milestone because, in our church, eight is the age at which we are baptized. I was thrilled to confirm and celebrate my relationship with God, not to mention show my family I mattered. Baptism was all we talked about in Primary class every Sunday for months.

Even for the Bagleys, birthdays meant there would be cake

and ice cream. Our family celebrated 11 birthdays throughout the year, so the promise of having ice cream nearly once a month loomed large in our minds. Even the older kids looked forward to celebrating together with genuine excitement.

The week before I turned eight, our cousin Jesse came to visit from Salt Lake City. His parents allowed him to stay overnight, then they would pick him up from Farm Creek to drive back to the city. Jesse was one of our city-dwelling cousins whose very presence in our rural home made me desperate to impress him. He was cool because he could ride a skateboard and everyone seemed to love him.

That Sunday, our mother sent the boys outside and asked the girls to help her in the kitchen. Because it was the Sabbath, she didn't assign us regular chores. The one exception was her expectation that we help her in the kitchen. For someone so help-lessly bad at cooking decent-tasting food, she had all sorts of opinions about how to cook the most bland, unappetizing food imaginable.

The boys used our time outside to ride bikes, play tag around the barns, and entertain each other for hours. As the afternoon progressed, we began to catch whiffs of a cake baking in the oven. I knew that the timing lined up with my birthday being only six days away. Though no one confirmed to me out loud that I would be the center of this celebration, the scent of cake-baking was the only information I needed.

Hours passed before Kate emerged from the kitchen to call us inside. My excitement had escalated by then because something told me this was going to be the best birthday celebration of my entire life!

The five of us boys—the four Bagley brothers and Jesse—burst through the back door toward the kitchen. We were greeted with homemade streamers hanging from the ceiling, and a cake with a dozen lit candles set as the centerpiece of the kitchen table. Everyone shouted, "Surprise!" producing a dazzling smile from me. I was radiating pure joy.

They all began to sing "Happy Birthday" in unison—or something like it. By the second verse, it was clear they were singing "Happy *Un*-Birthday," instead. I felt confused, but no less thrilled. It wasn't technically my birthday yet, so there was a considerable grace period for all celebrants to organize themselves around me. The song concluded, shocking me with a final message: "Happy *un*-birthday, dear Jesse, happy un-birthday to you!"

This party was never for me.

Jesse looked confused and embarrassed at first, pointing to himself and asking, "Me?" Everyone enthusiastically nodded and explained his un-birthday celebration. He seemed flattered and gracious about it, though still confused.

I was disappointed initially, but then I joined in the fun and lighthearted celebration. I told myself I had nothing to be sad about, given that my actual birthday was only six days away. We were still getting ice cream now, and we would also get to do this all over again in a few days!

Jesse returned home before I turned eight. When my birthday finally arrived, I was met with no celebration whatsoever. Everyone in my family wished me a happy birthday, but there was no cake, no ice cream, no presents, and no cards.

I asked Mom if we were going to have cake and ice cream for my birthday. She responded flatly, "We just did that on Sunday." I could feel my eyes rim with tears, though I did my best to conceal it. This felt completely unfair. Why had my family thrown such a big party for our cousin for his un-birthday, while no one thought to do that for my actual birthday?

Knowing I had no chance to win, I still chose to argue with our mother. "But it's my birthday," I said, trying not to sound like I was whining.

Mom looked at me squarely and said, "It's been a busy week and we just had cake and ice cream on Sunday. I haven't had a chance to even think about your birthday, so we'll do a combined birthday celebration for you and Ben this year."

Ben's birthday was a month and a half away from mine, which felt like an eternity at that moment. I wanted to punish her with my protest, but I could see from her expression that I didn't have a chance to drive home the point. Instead, I went to my room, buried my face in my pillow and cried.

————

Baptisms for children at our church in Roosevelt, Utah took place on the first Saturday of each month. I felt so excited, like I was starting to grow up. We drove to the church building, where Dad and I were fitted with white jumpers for the ceremony. There were several rows of children my age joining me to be baptized

We sang several hymns and heard from a few speakers, then took turns entering the baptismal font. Most of us followed the tradition of being baptized by our fathers. When it was my turn, Dad raised his arm to the square and recited the baptism prayer: "Calvin Dean Bagley, having been commissioned of Jesus Christ, I baptize you in the name of the Father, and of the Son and of the Holy Ghost. Amen."

I covered my mouth and nose with my hand as Dad gently lowered me beneath the water and brought me back up to the surface. When he smiled warmly at me and then hugged me tightly, I almost felt as if he loved me. I assumed that God had granted me this small act of kindness to transcend all of the harm my father was capable of doing.

I felt clean and deeply proud.

The following day, we completed the second part of the baptism ordinance, which is called *confirmation* in our church. At the front of the congregation, I sat in a chair while Dad and several other men of the church placed their hands on my head in prayer. Dad began, "Calvin Dean Bagley, in the name of Jesus Christ, and by the authority of the Melchizedek Priesthood, we lay our hands upon your head and confirm you as a member of the Church of Jesus Christ of Latter-day Saints, and say unto you, 'Receive the Holy Ghost.'"

With those words, I felt a warm glow emit from my heart. This was the first time in my life I felt the overwhelming presence of love and well-being. I understood then that there was something real and meaningful about my place in the church and with God. Though I was already beginning to recognize the hypocrisy in my parents' behavior, I was still able to understand that God was more powerful than that. I felt something that day —and for years that followed—that was bigger than them. Bigger than me.

By some miracle, I held onto that feeling throughout my life. There would be evidence I was on the right path all along, reminding me that someone or something had traveled the path before me. In my heart, that someone has always been God.

When Ben's birthday arrived a few weeks later, it was time for our alleged combined celebration. I had been looking forward to it, but reality, as it is wont to do, hardly matched up with my expectations. Once more, our family gathered around the kitchen table over cake and ice cream, everyone singing "Happy Birthday." But when they reached the end of the song, they only sang, "Happy Birthday, dear Ben, happy birthday to you." I sat dejected among my siblings as I watched Ben unwrap a few simple presents to end the celebration.

"You said Ben and I were going to combine our birthday celebrations," I said to Mom. She replied curtly, "I never said that. We celebrated your birthday a month ago. Don't you remember when Jesse was here?" I supposed it was too much to ask to remember to celebrate all nine children.

On my eighth un-birthday, I realized there was no point in arguing.

———

"Mom put *me* in charge, not you!" My older sister September shouts at Cynthia.

As my honorary mother, Cynthia defends her role as my protector, hands flying to her hips in defiance. Poor Belinda paces nervously behind our older sisters, eyes darting between the two.

I have always belonged to Cynthia. In every way, she was the mother in my life and I was her son. Whenever my older sisters fought, as they often did, I took my place on the stairs cordoned off from harm. I knew I shouldn't, but I played favorites with my siblings and Cynthia always won.

My adrenaline spikes as I boldly proclaim, "*Stop* being mean to Cynthee!" from my perch on the middle stairs. September pivots to attack me with three swift steps. She shoves her face as close to mine as she can without touching me, nostrils flaring.

"*Stay out of it.*"

I am three years old with no chance of winning an argument against someone 13 years my senior. Tears leap from my eyes as I crumple and fold into a heap of messy sobs.

I hate how she makes me feel.

But as much as I want to deny it, I know September is special. I concede this fact, even as my face grows hot with frantic tears.

September is the first person in our family who makes the piano really come alive for me. The way she commands the keys hypnotizes every one of us. Her fingers float effortlessly across the keys. Rhapsodies materialize each time she sits down to play. She creates beauty in a way I have never experienced before. I believe that God accompanies her as a gift to the rest of us. I often sidle next to her, mesmerized by how quickly her hands move without hesitation. Her eyes are fixed on the sheet music, never having to watch her hands to know which keys to play.

I once overheard my mother chatting about September on the phone with another mother from our church. She criticizes other pianists, opting instead to emphasize September's skills.

A narcissist sees her children's talents as an extension of her own, which therefore merit praise.

Early on in my childhood, Cynthia left for Provo—she was the first of us to attempt escape—taking her voice and little else with her in hopes of becoming a musician herself. She wrote to us about all of the talent surrounding her in the city, but we could read between the lines.

"It's different here," she wrote once. "Everyone's the best from somewhere." It was what she didn't say that told us she had given up.

As my sisters grew older, our living room gradually morphed into a sea of tissue paper, taffeta, sequins, stenciled patterns and scraps of fabric. They would excitedly gather to measure and cut confusing shapes from bright swaths of cloth. They huddled together over our dining table, tiny pins clenched between their teeth and measuring tape draped around their necks. Each sister took her turn as the mannequin propped in a fixed position, waiting for the other amateur ateliers to dress her. The sewing machine whirred well into the night, and most hurriedly before church dances.

Each of my sisters dazzled in her own way. Admittedly, my knowledge of fashion was limited, but their works of art seemed elaborate and sophisticated. Belinda's baby blue tunic with lace trim made her eyes shine so brightly they sparkled; September favored the emerald green dress she wore when she practiced her twirls like a debutante in the mirror.

An exciting energy buzzed through our house on dance nights. The older girls nervously chattered between our only bathroom and the hallway, trading places every few minutes to preen in front of the mirror.

I loitered curiously from a distance, reluctant to interrupt any of them. My heart clattered against my ribcage whenever the doorbell rang, a sure sign a date was there to whisk one of my sisters away.

"Hey, kid, beat it," one would say as he ruffled my hair.

I'd fade away slowly into the background, dragging my feet as I went. I longed to be part of this glamorous world I could not yet touch.

I wanted my chance to make-believe.

———

The chapel pews in the Tridell church smell of pine trees and lemon. I fidget with our hymnal, bored already by Wade's homecoming speech. Belinda seems nervous—she's already applied her lipstick twice before grabbing her mirror for another inspection. September repeatedly tucks a strand of hair behind her ear to quiet her nerves.

Wade is the only one of us who doesn't appear nervous. He stands confidently at the podium, recounting stories about his mission. I make no attempts to pay attention, except when September stops my little legs mid-swing, forcing my feet to dangle with no place to go.

I notice how sly Wade is when he brushes his arm discreetly across September's. He beams having September standing next to him in what has become a receiving line for well-wishers. His hand barely touches her elbow, and blush appears on her cheekbones as if painted there.

He relishes all the attention, that much is obvious. He has a way of staring at each member of our family as if he were the sole judge of a pageant and we are his contestants. His eyes lazily take in our motley crew before they land on me. He glowers with scorn moments before I hide behind Cynthia's skirt. When he catches my eyes like that, something unnatural flickers behind his. It's hard to know whether I am me, or if I am prey. The uncertainty disturbs me in and of itself. I think if I knew the answer, I wouldn't like it.

———

When Belinda was 19 years old, she broke free to the youth-filled city of Provo, Utah.

One evening, she was driving at sunset. The sun was blinding, which made her squint hard through the windshield. She maintained a temperate speed, knowing there were pedestrians on the moderately busy street. Moments after entering the street, a family turned to walk on the sidewalk a few yards away, having just left church for a funeral.

An old woman walked with the family, unaware of how close she was to the street. With one small step off the curb, the old woman stumbled into Belinda's blind spot. The sun shrouded the old woman, blocking her entirely from view. Belinda had no time to swerve before she struck the old woman in the middle of a residential street. The entire family witnessed the accident, their faces twisted with horror.

The woman died on her way to the hospital.

Belinda called home immediately and told our parents what had happened. I recall my mother unceremoniously telling us that Belinda had killed an old woman and might be charged with vehicular manslaughter. When we tried to pump more information out of our mother, she just kept repeating that she "had a bad feeling" about Belinda moving to Provo.

This—like all tragedies that befell her and others—was foreseeable, foretold only by a spirit whose warning she had ignored.

Back in the 1980s, landlines required paying extra for dialing out to "long distance" numbers that might be only a few miles away. And because calls to and from Provo were too expensive for us, we were not able to communicate with Belinda very much. She was alone and terrified in a city much too big for her comfort. She had no idea what to do, so she went to our grandma and grandpa's house in Salt Lake City. They tried to give her the attention she needed, but they were not in a position to have any one of their dozens of grandchildren stay with them for an extended period of time. But our grandparents were so good to us, and I loved them deeply. They allowed her to stay for a few days in their basement guest bedroom.

The old woman's family did not press charges. The police found it to be an unfortunate accident without fault. Though horrific and shocking in and of itself, I am more dumbstruck by my parents' lack of reaction than I am of the accident itself. My mother and father left their daughter alone in Salt Lake City to navigate the legal system by herself, knowing she might be facing a long prison sentence as a result.

Not long after the accident, Belinda met Gaylord "Joe" Stotts, a chain-smoking, thrice-divorced man over a decade older than her. He had jet-black hair and a big, bushy black mustache that completely swallowed his upper lip. He was short and stout and pleasant enough, cigarette smoke notwithstanding.

Joe was a spectacle—a hypnotist who was excommunicated from the church for being unfaithful to his recent wife. Belinda fell in love with him, somehow, and was excited to bring him home to meet our parents. You could tell he tried to cover up the smell of cigarette smoke that clung to his clothes, but he reeked of it.

Moreover, he could not make it through one evening at our house without taking several smoke breaks. I'm not sure if that said more about him or our family.

He promised our father that he was going to clean up his act, presumably speaking to a forgiving audience after we gathered for evening family prayer. He claimed he wanted to quit smoking and work with a bishop to be re-baptized into the church. To make matters worse, he began to sweat profusely as if he were melting right there in our living room. He continued to sweat and stutter through the evening, filtering in and out of our house.

After we said our goodbyes, he and Belinda walked out to his red four-door Subaru to "get something from the car." I followed them outside, my nose instantly inhaling a trail of fresh cigarette smoke in the air. "I needed a smoke break," he chuckled to me, "after I promised your dad I would quit smoking and marry your sister the 'right way.'"

————

Blaine was Wade's half-brother. I was about 12 when he moved in with September and Wade, though I know he and September were at each other's throats. When things became too combustible at their place, he moved in with us. It was very exciting at first to have a 20-something in the house, especially one as talented as Blaine. He had an incredible singing voice, owned a car, and enjoyed money he got from the Ute tribe each month.

Blaine was not the first—nor would he be the last—to sexually abuse someone in our family. My siblings and I were little more than prey to him.

He hopped between our houses every couple of months. One day, September walked into her baby's room, startling him. She caught him touching the baby inappropriately while changing her diaper. She kicked him out immediately, but the only place he had to go was our house. My parents ignored her warnings. They didn't believe her because they always believed September to be too dramatic.

I know now that the stories Blaine told me were important components of his grooming process. One story in particular almost made me happy I wasn't in school—something about boys dropping their pants for the school nurse trying to hide their hard-ons. How embarrassing, I thought.

Some of my memories are hazier than I'm comfortable admitting, but I remain grateful for that. Though I am not always conscious of doing it, I've learned that some of my most painful memories hide themselves from my consciousness, allowing me to survive without my nervous system shutting down. My theory is that the human body's reaction to trauma offers tender mercies, our own physiology alleviating suffering during a traumatic experience. I think about people who are trapped in a burning building, dying of smoke inhalation rather than suffering the excruciating pain of burning alive. Similarly, when we break a bone, the body goes into shock, warding off immediate pain by blocking those receptors in our brain. There seems to be an intelligent creation in our design—further evidence of God's grace.

I remember being outside with Blaine near the front bridge, the ditch just beneath us. He grabbed one of our black cats that suddenly appeared, flipping it over to expose its stomach. He began to slowly pantomime then actually massage its penis. He chortled maniacally as if this were the funniest thing he'd ever seen.

One day, Uvene and my mother were relaxing in the living room. Out of nowhere, Uvene flipped over to her tummy, rubbing herself back and forth on the carpet. My mother gasped, then quickly chided Uvene to stop at once. Many years later, mom asked me if I thought Blaine had touched Uvene. I bit my tongue to stop myself from screaming *"of course"* in her clueless face. What did she think was going to happen? Fate kept tabs on our limited chances at avoiding harm, its calls to humble us an extortionate demand.

———

Jeff begged our parents to expel Blaine, but his pleas fell on deaf ears, so he called Cynthia—our forever protector. She was living in Salt Lake City and had just begun her military service, but she dropped everything to come to Farm Creek to help us.

She arrived that afternoon, unannounced. Dad was in the garden and hadn't yet realized she was there. I was beside myself with excitement as I saw her car pull off the highway in front of our house. She stepped out, barely making eye contact. "Where is Blaine?" she asked, almost brushing me aside.

Confused, I told her he had gone into town. "I need to talk to Jeff," she said firmly, and quickly went inside the house.

She spent the afternoon with Jeff, and I began to feel completely overlooked. I was hurt, but I didn't yet understand why. My young mind had come to see her as my mother—and now, she wasn't giving me the attention she once had. I begged her to spend time with me, but she replied that Jeff needed her more right now, and that we'd have plenty of time together soon.

She was on a holy mission.

Cynthia is a spiritualist who believes she possesses sacred power. Her power isn't recognized as divine by the formal structures of the church, but she believes in it all the same. Her ways of worship are holy to her.

That night, she and Jeff went outside together in the dark. Later, she told me how they sat barefoot on the front lawn, dropping into a deep meditative state. She gripped the grass like strands of hair, as if pulling something from the earth itself. With one hand held to the sky, she prayed fervently to Mother Earth—gathering energy from the ground beneath her and directing it toward healing our family.

The next morning, Cynthia sat down with my mother and tried to explain that Blaine had given himself over to a particular kind of evil. Mid-sentence, Blaine poked his head into the living room. "I have to leave immediately," he said. I followed him to the car, hoping this time it was real. "Your sister is a witch!" he exclaimed, slamming the door. "I have to get out of here."

Two weeks later, he returned—but this time he never made it across the bridge to our front lawn.

"Is your dad home?" he asked from beside his car. Dad was in the garden, tilling the soil as he always did. Still, Blaine waited by the car, not daring to move until Dad came over to meet him. I lingered nearby, hidden from view, straining to hear their exchange.

What followed was a jumble of apologies and vague confessions—word salad that would have confused anyone who didn't already know what Blaine was sorry for. Dad didn't. He nodded along, accepting the apology, unaware of its weight. I feared they might reconcile, that Blaine would once again step inside our house. But he never crossed the bridge.

After a few minutes of awkward conversation, he got back in his car and drove off down the country highway.

The next day, he hanged himself.

———

Years later, I would sit in September and Wade's living room in Whiterocks as Wade played a handmade cedar flute. Wade would lift the flute to his lips and coax out sounds that mystified his listeners. September would harmonize, her voice clear and elegant. They'd recorded three CDs by then, their image appearing in the local paper, both of them donning traditional Ute clothing. Wade's face was fixed with a stoic expression, September's hair was fixed in braids.

The store they'd opened in Roosevelt—Redstone Music—had a bell that chimed when customers entered; sheet music lined the walls and guitars hung by their necks.

September had grown cautious and paranoid since she'd married Wade. "People would rather drive 40 miles to Vernal than buy anything from Indians." Her arguments were only ever rhetorical—conspiracies that moved like the truth. Wade rolled his eyes behind her back. He liked to display his lack of loyalty to her or anyone, as long as there was an audience. It didn't matter if they agreed privately; he was prone to forgetting their common ground. September fought his battles so he could keep his hands clean. He liked to play the good guy.

I never stopped vying for his attention or approval. One night, he presented my older brother Jeff with a rifle and some clothing. Jeff loved to hear Wade describe how much he "reminded him of himself at that age." I squirmed with every empty compliment directed at my brother. I invited myself into the conversation, stuttering about hunting and camping.

"Do you ever stop talking?" Wade spewed. "You're going to be the weatherman on TV someday. Always talking and never saying anything." His words curdled in the air. I did not dare respond. He chuckled to himself, repeating the thought: "Always talking, never saying anything." My stomach dropped when September laughed, too, grateful not to be the target of his derision.

Wade was a slippery shapeshifter who moved too easily between the ideal missionary speaking in reverent tones and the wise medicine man recounting stories of ceremonies and vision quests. His words slowly poisoned September against the rest of us, a fact that would later shield him from culpability. His presence is burned in my memory as an otherworldly phenomenon.

At night, I'd sometimes peer around shadowy corners expecting him to appear. To me, he was like the skinwalker of Ute lore, hoping to kill me in my sleep.

"Adults are the real monsters," I breathed, trying not to fear the dark.

"Looks like we can use this space," Ed said, both of us standing in the attic of the dusty storage shed, craning our necks toward the rafters above. "Nobody else is."

Jeff nodded, already measuring dimensions mentally as he replied, "Dad might let us have it."

When my brothers approached our father that evening, he barely acknowledged them. "Use what space you want. Just don't burn the place down."

Ed and Jeff spent the next two weeks scavenging for scraps from behind our barn. Hammering and sawdust filled the shed as they transformed weathered planks, bent nails and thick leather straps from an old harness into sound construction. They managed to build a wooden door that groaned and creaked loudly on its leather hinges. The sound of the door swinging shut marked this space as their exclusive portal.

It was a very tight space burrowed in the attic of a storage shed where we kept all of our canned food and a potato cellar. The entry was miniature, forcing us to crawl in on our hands and knees. There wasn't enough room for us to stand up, but it was more than enough for us simply because it was ours.

They christened it "The Hut" with such pomp and circumstance it was as if they were knights in King Arthur's court surveying their kingdom. Inside the space, they built crude bed frames on either side of the sloped walls to hold their sleeping bags with a narrow walkway down the middle for guests. Jeff rigged a black PVC pipe to snake itself from the back corner down through a hole in the roof, an ingenious solution to clandestine nighttime bathroom trips.

When Jeff's friend Troy started sleeping over at The Hut, I'd squeeze myself beside the doors with my knees tucked tightly against my chest, listening to their older boy conversations and feeling grateful to almost be included.

Ed mysteriously acquired a wooden crate filled with dozens of candles that were now ours to decorate. They burned for hours, dripping wax onto the floorboard in smatterings of patterns, filling up the cramped and sacred space with the smell of melted paraffin.

Then one night, everything changed.

Ed leaned close toward Jeff and I, whispering, "Want to see something?" Of course we did.

He took a gratuitous length of time to display a colorful box hidden beneath his sleeping bag. There, amongst the dancing shadows in the candlelight, lay the forbidden contraband: *Monopoly*.

Our father hated the game that valorized capitalism. "The love of money is the root of all evil. That game teaches greed and corruption," he would warn. And yet, there it was—the colorful

Monopoly board, a forbidden item like Dungeons & Dragons, a pair of shorts or even a Coca-Cola.

"Please don't tell," Jeff pleaded with me, his eyes growing wide and earnest. "We promise to let you play if you keep this secret." I stared at the box with conflicting feelings surging within me. Part of me was prepared to climb down the ladder and run straight into our house to tell Dad. But the bigger part of me—the one that felt certain I could manage a secret—made me nod in agreement.

"I promise. I won't tell a soul."

————

From that night forward, I basked in the glow of our unsanctioned malfeasance. We'd tacitly agree to wait until the house grew dark, or until we could hear Dad's heavy snoring through his open bedroom window. Then we'd light our candles like watchmen patrolling a cemetery on the graveyard shift. The board beckoned to us with its vibrant colors and unclaimed real estate, all of its properties creating our very own miniature city ripe for the taking—Park Place and Boardwalk, Reading Railroad and Baltic Avenue.

One night, I found myself in the middle of a complex trade. "I'll trade you St. Charles Place for your orange spot," I offered. Jeff countered, "No way. But I'll give you Tennessee for two hundred, cash."

No sooner had I greedily reached for the bills did we hear our father's gruff voice from below: "What are you kids doing? You are supposed to be in bed!" Instinctively, I held my breath. We heard him below and wondered how long he had been listening.

"We're just up here, talking, but we'll go to bed. Sorry, Dad." Jeff's voice came out with a steady assurance, reminding us how he could always stay calm under pressure.

At any moment, our father could climb the ladder to our cove and see the little metal shoe sitting on Marvin Gardens. "It's past your bedtime," he huffed. "Put out the candles before you go to bed." And with that, we heard his footsteps retreat back toward the house.

We sat stunned waiting for the slam of our house door as our permission to speak again. But none of us dared to break the silence.

I slept fitfully that night, tossing and turning with thoughts of our father losing his temper and taking out his rage and disappointment on us. He was so unpredictable in the way he meted out punishment. Would we receive a lecture or a beating, or both?

He had an excellent imagination.

I was grateful that we had the foresight to hide the game before we went to sleep. We folded the colorful board with solemnity, bundling paper money with rubber bands and gathering metal tokens to place in their designated slots. All of our joy packed into itself so easily, I wondered if we would ever get to play again.

That afternoon, we passed the time as we always did: by doing dozens of chores. As I helped Mom with laundry in the house, I spotted Dad climbing the ladder to The Hut. He moved swiftly and seemingly with purpose, which made my stomach knot as I watched from the window helplessly.

Twenty minutes passed before he climbed back down the ladder.

Once it was safe to do reconnaissance, I made my way stealthily to the scene of the crime. I knew before I reached the top of the ladder what had transpired there. Our father had pried up all of the floorboards, one nail at a time. His heavy footprints were visible in the sawdust scattered on the floor, like a crime scene dusted for prints. Through the door, I could see smoke rising from the burn barrel behind our house. The air was thick with acrid smoke, the scent of burning cardboard and melting plastic choking the fresh air.

That was the day our father murdered fun. Our Monopoly board was gone forever.

Inside The Hut, the only thing present at the center of the floor was the game box lid. Dad had left it behind on purpose. He had to leave his mark.

I picked up the lid with both hands, admiring the familiar artwork with a new sense of nostalgia. It was then that I noticed for the first time that the box lid contained a perfectly crafted miniature replica of the entire Monopoly board, complete with all the properties, railroads and corner squares.

From there, I decided to make something out of this nothing.

I crept up and down the stairs slowly, avoiding the spots on the wooden planks I knew would groan loudest. Avoiding detection, I safely grabbed what I needed. I doubled back to The Hut, hiding a pair of scissors under my shirt. I began carefully cutting along the edges of the printed board, separating the replica cleanly from the cardboard.

Once I was finished, I looked around the empty Hut with satisfaction. I tucked the six-inch board replica beneath my shirt.

Some games, I decided, were worth playing no matter who set the rules.

4. STAKE DANCES AND FALSE PROPHETS

"Prayer time."

We bowed our heads. Dad's voice, moments ago hollering obscenities at our mother's departing car, now softened into a reverent tone.

"Dear Heavenly Father, we thank thee for this day and for our many blessings"

I peeked through my folded hands at Jeff, whose smirk was already visible. Kate stared at her folded hands solemnly, as if she might will herself to disappear.

"in the name of Jesus Christ, amen."

"Amen," we said in unison.

We watched as our father looked on in consternation, drumming his fingers on the table absently. He seemed uncomfortable and out of sorts. His jaw tightened as if he were chewing something tough. Without warning, he scraped back his chair and stormed off to the bathroom.

We heard him slam cabinet doors, then his heavy footsteps returning. He emerged with a deadly straight face clutching... toilet paper.

"Your mother," Dad began, his voice oddly tight and forcibly modulated, "has informed me that all of you are using too much toilet paper."

My eyes immediately cut to Jeff; his eyebrows shot up. Kate's chin nearly hit the table. It was not clear—not in the way that I needed it to be—whether or not my father was serious.

Once I heard him use the word "behinds" in earnest, I thought I might lose my composure. He said it almost gently as if none of us had just heard him call our mother a bitch while invoking God's name in vain mere minutes ago.

I didn't *think* Dad could read my thoughts, though I acted as if he could. I took precautions by not being too critical of him in moments of heightened emotional tension, which this display seemed to be turning into.

Dad set the roll of toilet paper on the table next to the scriptures. He tore off exactly four squares from the roll with dramatic flair. He then flipped open the Bible to search for the basis of his next lesson:

"Leviticus," he announced, stabbing the page with his finger. "Chapter 11, verses 32 through 40. Instructions about washing items—or body parts—that come into contact with unclean things."

Jeff and I shot each other confused glances. If I was to understand my father correctly, he was using the Old Testament to preach about the efficacy and frugality of wiping our butts properly.

"Four squares," he announced, holding them up for us to examine. "No more. No less."

He stood up for his soliloquy. This was his big moment.

"First, you take your four squares," he continued, demonstrating by holding the paper away from his body, "and you wipe *thoroughly* the first time." He moved his hand in a swift, purposeful motion that made all three of us lean back in our chairs.

"Next," he said, his voice gaining the fervor of a tent revival preacher, "you fold it over, and you wipe again, *like so*."

If a stranger had walked into our home at this very moment, they would have found my father in a most compromised position. He had committed his whole body to the motion, his signature Levi's 501 jeans stretching taut across his thighs as he bent slightly forward—for maximum effect.

He was a vision.

Kate made a sound somewhere between a cough and a wheeze. Jeff bit his lower lip so hard I thought he might draw blood. I stared at the Bible, wondering if anywhere in its holy pages there was guidance for this particular moment. I was sure I would burst from holding in my laughter.

"Your mother will not—I repeat, *will not*—speak to me about toilet paper again," Dad declared, crumpling the demonstration pieces and tossing them toward the trash can.

I think the waste was lost on him, but I kept that thought to myself.

Dad stood there, his hands on his hips, surveying the faces of his mortified children. It was clear he felt proud and mighty. He was a man who had negotiated personal hygiene with four squares of toilet paper, all while invoking biblical authority.

The Way, The Truth and the Two-Ply.

I bit the inside of my cheek, suppressing the laughter that threatened to explode from me. "Now then," Dad said, settling back into his squeaky chair and opening his scriptures. "Let's return to our reading."

———

My father put an awful lot of trust in God. To him, no one could be trusted *but* God.

He corralled us daily, his willing captives, suffocating us with protracted three-hour lectures around family prayers. It was during these divinely sanctioned Bagley summits that he taught us about the rules and regulations we needed to follow to live in a God-like way. He modeled for us with his own behavior, proving to us that these were the conditions we had to meet for God to bestow His love on us. When we complied, we were in His—and his—favor.

Our father modeled exactly how we were to pray. By his hand, we approached prayer together in a reflexive and rigid way. Our group prayer time was comprehensive: morning family prayer, evening family prayer and a blessing before each meal. We formed a circle in the living room, folding our heads and bowing.

At mealtime, we took turns leading the prayer, rotating from oldest to youngest. When it was one of our parents' turns to lead the prayer, we all shifted uncomfortably in position; we knew we might as well make ourselves comfortable for the lengthy monologue ahead, and the chapped, numbed kneecaps left once our kneeling was done.

I sensed his prayers were heartfelt; I knew his relationship with God was more than just supplication. But despite his sincerity, his prayers also served as tools for manipulation, subtle criticism and pointed commentary about our listening skills.

We were expected to listen and not speak, whether that meant through prayer or parental conditioning. And no matter how long it took us to perfect, my father expected our souls to be purified before our heads hit the pillow. The one snag in his methods was the constancy of his and our mother's fighting. There were times when their punctuated hollers carried on past midnight, ensuring our sleep would be postponed until he could approve our form.

When I was in primary class at church, I made a prayer rock inscribed with a poem. Its words instructed me to place the rock on my pillow before I fell asleep so that when my head landed I would be reminded with blunt force to pray before slumbering. In the morning, I placed the rock slightly under my bed so that I'd stub my toe as a reminder I needed to start my day with prayer.

Though my logic was faulty at best, I found an enormous

amount of peace using it in my private prayer practice. This was a ritual of my own that I could control without the prying eyes of my parents or my siblings.

The Church of Jesus Christ of Latter-day Saints (LDS) structures itself with church bodies that are formed into "wards" by geographic regions. A "stake" is the umbrella term for a collection of wards.

In our rural area of the Uintah Basin, our fellow parishioners were so few that our congregation amounted to a "branch"—too infinitesimal and isolated, even for normal worship. In addition to perfect attendance at Sunday worship, my father aspired to be like the LDS scholars he studied.

He wrote two books, neither of which could pass muster in any conceivable way. In the texts, he twisted scripture to suit his style of discipline and made spurious claims about prophecies that never occurred. When presented with the opportunity to meet one of his favorite authors, W. Cleon Skousen, my father promptly thrust one of his own crudely written books at his hero. Skousen carefully perused the text, out of politeness more than anything, eventually breaking it to my father that his book contained false doctrine.

My father's book excoriated LDS church members for not being sufficiently reliant on the Lord. He bemoaned their over-reliance on self rather than God citing the 2 Chronicles 32:8 "the arm of flesh," something he lectured about frequently. At this rejection, he experienced a tinge of humiliation briefly, though only moments later he decided that his version of God's way was the incontrovertible truth.

Skousen was wrong.

As a child, few things made me more uneasy than our Monday night meetings, or Family Home Evenings, an LDS family tradition akin to a family council. My parents insisted that our family gather to discuss the gospel and to (theoretically) do enjoyable activities together. I recall neither the earnest group study of the scriptures nor the inveterate fun activities to follow.

My mother insisted we center our focus on reviewing the family calendar. What—I have never once ascertained—did my parents allow us to do in the first place? We were all puzzled, week after week, nodding absently at her ambition.

We didn't socialize with neighbors because we didn't have any; Ute native people within a ten-mile radius looked at us as interlopers on stolen land. We didn't have classmates because we did not attend school. There were no bake sales or sports events to crowd our weekend days. Even if there were rec leagues to join, our parents wouldn't dare expose us to those kids and their worldly ways.

Once we finished our performative review of the family schedule, our father would lead us in scripture readings. He was partial to the language of barbarism in the Old Testament or prophesies of the End of Times in Revelations, conveniently glossing over Jesus's message of unconditional love and forgiveness found in the New Testament and the Book of Mormon. He quickly became pedantic and almost angry as he worked himself into a spiritual lather, whether he was quoting Numbers or Deuteronomy. He always followed the same order: an opening hymn, the opening prayer, a calendar review, a lesson on the gospel, a closing song and a closing prayer—all culminating in a promised treat that never materialized.

By the time he delivered his last impassioned plea to us sinners, it was time to go to bed, lest we forget our bedtime prayers. Though the LDS church tradition of family home evenings invited joy and happiness, we rarely experienced such contentment. Our gatherings reminded me of a joke I learned playing basketball at a church league: *The fight that begins with a prayer.*

I was never more aware of my illiteracy or my brothers' than when our family studied scripture together. There were flashes of shame I saw when my brother, Jeff, stumbled over his words with every sentence he struggled to read out loud.

Despite the obvious gaps in our skills—specifically for my

brothers and me—our father insisted we each read ten verses, regardless of how difficult that often was. He was not manipulative enough for this to be an overt or intentional act of cruelty on his part. It's more likely that his pathological need to dominate overshadowed the bottomless needs of his brood. I don't think he ever once noticed.

The difficulty of the readings was not eased by my father's frequent interruptions. He could hardly contain himself. With each interjection, we would all stare downward, always wishing to be elsewhere. We were deliberate in our facial expressions because we didn't ever want to provoke his anger.

The problem with our father being unbridled in this way—unlimited in his influence over spiritual hostages—meant he would drone on for hours. He was less interested in bestowing loving instruction and more focused on hellfire and damnation. Worse still, he chose these times to hijack scripture study to divert our focus on how bereft his children were of discipline and respect. His admonitions about our lack of work ethic, honor toward our parents and our general existence were nothing more than a shibboleth, shallow in their dubious ties to the loving words of scripture.

———

When I was five years old, my father sustained a near-catastrophic injury at work.

While checking the pressure gauge on his truck, he climbed onto a stool, leaning in face-first to inspect the tank. When he gripped the hatch handle, a giant explosion threw him backward into the air. His body hit the ground with a violent thud, and blood quickly spread from underneath his head.

Co-workers who heard the blast rushed over to him, their voices urgently barking instructions while overlapping each other. The explosion was so severe, they thought he might be dead.

He came home from the hospital a few days after the accident. He was hard to look at. His left cheek had swollen to twice its normal size, his skin was painted a deep purple-black. After he returned home, he was immobilized for weeks. Time passed slowly as he tossed and turned in his bed, sheets twisting around his limbs and empty plates stacking themselves along his nightstand.

After what felt like months, my father suddenly emerged from his cave. He looked gaunt, his expression vacant. He had lost an enormous amount of weight, and I barely recognized him. But I still felt grateful he was alive. That day, and for many days after, his work clothes hung untouched in the closet.

That was the last time I remember seeing my father work a real job.

———

As a teenager, I remember vividly the night Dad joined me on the porch to tell me *something important*.

He sat on the steps slowly and heavily, as if to underscore the situation's gravity. He kept silent for a few moments before he began.

"I could never satisfy your mother," he declared flatly, no context given.

"She'd wait for me at the door, ready to attack me when I got home from work. The first thing she'd do was pound both of her fists against my chest, shouting, 'More money! We need more money. More money. *More money!*'"

His fingers absently traced the fading scars on his cheek as he spoke. "We needed more money," he repeated, more to himself than to me.

I sat there, stunned. Memories of our empty pantry, the barely functional outhouse in the backyard and our cut-off electricity flooded my mind. Mom was right; we needed more money.

In light of this new information, mornings in church with my father became especially uncomfortable. I shifted uneasily in the pew each time the bishop gave a talk about God's expectations of parents: the father's duty to provide for his family, the mother's duty to look after the children and keep the home. I stole glances at my father during these speeches that were clearly meant for him. I waited for him to flinch, but his expression never changed.

Years later, my father's selective amnesia and revisionist history formed the dominant narrative of our childhood. He'd lean back in his chair, waving his hand dismissively at any one of us, boys or girls. "I watched you girls slave away in that kitchen," he'd say. "I stopped working so I could push your mother to work, for *your* sake." His eyes wandered around, avoiding our eyes when he lied. He looked distant and troubled, and his words made compassion difficult for me.

Cynthia has since told me she remembers the morning Dad walked into the kitchen, Mom dutifully washing the dishes. "I'm done," he declared, his voice and face affectless. "I'm done providing."

My mother scrubbed the last surface of a large plate before she put it on the drying rack gently. Her hands still wet with soapy water, she replied, "How are we going to afford food? How will we afford clothes for the kids?"

He shrugged, then turned toward the bedroom to dismiss himself. He took each step gingerly, replying to the walls: "We don't need any of that stuff. If you want it so badly, then you can get it yourselves." And with that, he slammed the bedroom door shut, mumbling to himself.

Later that night, I caught a glimpse of my fractured reflection in the mirror hanging behind my parents' bedroom door. The cheap, bowed mirror we bought from Kmart had cracked for possibly the last time before it would surely break for good.

My parents fought so often and with such aggression that the mirror itself was the most obvious casualty of their violent fights. For many years, I have fixated over the reflection of myself I saw that night in that mirror, staring back at me like a multi-faceted monster.

Though I had not broken anything or anyone, I still felt ashamed. More than anything, what hung before me was over-whelming evidence of my fractured childhood. The way I saw myself was accurate, if not abhorrent. I did not cause the pain I felt—I could not have; I witnessed it, and would never be able to unsee it. The message I had internalized so deeply all these years was that I was born wicked, and all of the typical growing pains that come along with childhood were, to my parents, all signs pointing toward a son who needed to be disciplined through vituperative words and deeds.

For the next three days, our father did not come out of his room. Our mother paced the kitchen floor in her fuzzy slippers, making the creepy shuffling sounds of a much older woman traversing the linoleum. I heard her lift the receiver two or three times before she started dialing numbers. It sounded like she was talking to either relatives or friends in Vernal, and it seemed like that had made her feel better. After she placed her last call, she changed into one of the few dresses she owned, applying lipstick. Moments later, she whisked herself away for job interviews.

The Basin Nickel Ads was a local advertising company that offered her a sales job for commission-only pay. I remember her seeming stressed out when she opened those first few paychecks, assuming by her expression they did not amount to much.

Over time, those payments grew. Two years later, she had surpassed our father with her earning capacity.

Our lifestyle didn't change much. We still ate homegrown potatoes and prepared homemade bread. The bills continued to pile up on the kitchen counter. Our mother would hold her hand to her forehead, closing her eyes tightly. "It will be either the IRS or the bank that takes this house," she warned us, pointing her finger as if to accuse.

By the time I was 11 years old, my older siblings had moved out, leaving roughly half of our family whose mouths needed to be fed one way or another. It mattered little by whom.

————

I can't decide which chore I hate more: shelling peas, stuffing and sewing dinosaurs or folding fliers. Our crew of laborers canned thousands of Kerr jars of produce every season. But, shelling peas requires so much work and yields so little food.

A good portion of Mom's thousands and thousands of Kerr jars came from Wilma. After her demise in the car accident, her family cleared out her canned food stash. She had over 2,000 Kerr jars with rotten food in them, a massive collection she had accumulated over a lifetime. All of the food was expired by the time they discovered her stockpile.

Her son, who lived next to her, gave our family dozens of boxes of spoiled canned food so that we could use the jars. We emptied each and every one into a huge pile of preserves for composting. We sanitized the jars and stored them above the pumphouse where they would live until we started canning in the fall.

After Wilma died, Mom never had to purchase a single Kerr jar again.

————

"Cut along the lines," our mother shouts over the noise of her sewing machine. She points to paper patterns littering our kitchen table. "And make sure they are exact. We can't waste any material on your mistakes."

I cut slowly at first, making sure my scissors follow the dotted lines exactly. My siblings and I cut out green and brown dinosaur shapes. Once we sew all the basic pieces together, our real work begins.

I push my hand deep inside the pocket forming between the sewn flaps, trying to flip the correct pieces right-side-out. My fingers are not graceful. I am not coordinated.

But this is hungry work.

I grab fistfuls of white batting, carefully smushing the fluff into narrow openings: arms, legs, tails. We keep stuffing until each dinosaur feels plump and dense. There are hundreds of these prehistoric creations piled in front of us on the table and beside us on the floor. I don't feel proud of the hard work I've done—my eyelids are too heavy with fatigue.

Then there are the rock dinosaurs.

Our entire family piles into the back of our truck and rides until we stop at a dry creek bed where the desert heat shimmers like a mirage off the sand. "Look for the round ones to make their bodies," Mom demands. I dig and I dig and I dig—through collections of river rocks, through fingernails peeling themselves off the tips of my nailbeds.

The flat rocks we use for dinosaur heads are much harder to find. It is a small relief when we stumble upon an abundance of "spine" rocks: jagged pieces that bite into my palm as I clutch them tightly by the handful.

When we open the door to our house, the smell of hot glue wafts through the air. We immediately begin assembling our stone dinosaurs, then paint each of their faces with tiny brush-strokes: two black dots for eyes and a red line turned up for a mouth. Rows and rows of finished dinosaurs cover every visible surface.

On one such occasion, a photographer for the *Vernal Express* visits our production line. "Everyone smile," Mom says through gritted teeth. We arrange ourselves with the tallest of us in the back and the shorter ones in the front, the group of us flanked by hundreds of cloth dinosaurs it took us weeks to create.

The camera flash temporarily blinds me and I see squiggles

float across my vision for the next few minutes. Later, when the newspaper article runs, Mom shows us, with a huge sense of pride. She pulls out that article to show neighbors and friends many times over the years. On the main copy she still keeps at home, the words "local entrepreneur" are underlined twice.

There is no mention of the little hands that produced those dinosaurs at scale.

———

Folding fliers is a game of quickness and quantity rather than patience.

My shoulders already ache, and we've barely started. I stack two cardboard boxes in front of me to create a wobbly makeshift table for myself. The first box of fliers mocks me with its fullness, thousands of identical sheets waiting for my small hands to transform them into glossy tri-folds.

"Don't get sloppy with the folding," Mom calls from the kitchen. "My boss said the inserter jammed twice last week."

I nod without looking up, fanning a stack of papers between my thumb and forefinger. The edges nip at my skin. I've lost count of my papercuts. I try not to stare too long through the single window, silently begging another beautiful day outside not to pass us by.

Ben is already flying through his own stack. We work in harmony, with efficiency. The room falls silent, except for the soft flutter of sheets sliding against each other and thumbs smoothing the creases of the next flier up.

"How many boxes are left?" I ask, trying hard not to whine.

"Mind your business and do your job," my father insists. "We've got 23, maybe 24 on hand. Your mother is bringing more from town."

I quickly do the math. Twenty-four boxes means we won't finish until midnight. I wait as long as I can stand before I glance up at the clock—9:17 am.

We clocked in at sunrise to start our other chores. The goats were more tolerable this morning than usual. One of our most important tasks is to bottle-feed them, which we've done for every single one of them since birth. Dad reminds us that bottle-fed goats are saleable goods in the farming world, so it's our responsibility to make sure they are fed accordingly.

I resign myself to a very long day ahead. The next moment, I'm back to my rhythm: grab, fold, press, stack. Grab, fold, press, stack.

"Remember when Jeff used to race us?" Ben murmurs, "Hundred fliers in one minute?"

"Yeah. But he's gone now." My voice comes out harsher than intended. "We do his share, too."

We break only for water and to make peanut butter sandwiches, eaten with one hand while the other continues folding. My fingers are cramping up and my spirit is winding down. I'm so tired of working against my will.

When Mom's car crunches on the gravel outside, we all hold our breath.

"My boss needs these by tomorrow morning," she announces as she walks in. "I told him we'd manage."

My stomach sinks. Rather than helping us fold fliers, she retires to her room to rest—as if she's left her children doing homework, not laboring like factory workers.

Her justification is always that she did the work of selling to clients, so it is up to us to do the work of folding the fliers. After all, she needed her beauty rest to look bright-eyed and bushy-tailed to greet future clients the next day.

I excuse myself to the bathroom by pretending my fingers are bleeding again. On my way, I catch sight of the newspaper clipping Mom has framed on the wall—all nine of us kids smiling behind a mountain of cloth dinosaurs. "Local Mother's Homemade Dinosaurs a Hit with Tourists!" the headline reads. Babies making toys for babies.

In the bathroom, I run cold water over my hands. I like to

watch otherwise invisible paper cuts reveal themselves under the faucet stream. I ignore the mirror just above my eyeline— lately I don't recognize myself. I splash water on my face and wonder how many more thousand folds remain, how many hours of my childhood lost to strangers.

———

At 14, I was finally considered old enough to go to church dances, otherwise known as stake dances. A stake is a grouping of churches based on geographic proximity, which meant there would be an exponential number of girls. Jeff took me to one such dance in Vernal where he planned to meet up with Crystal. Taking up with Crystal was Jeff's ticket out of our family once and for all. She was cool enough, at least for introducing me to her friend who was closer to my age.

I took the liberty of calling this new girl my girlfriend, though I had no clue what that meant. I saw her a few more times, including at Crystal's 16th birthday party.

The first time I met her, I got her phone number. I was proud of that, but I did not think it through. I had to beg my parents just to talk to her for five minutes without incurring long distance charges. Unlike smartphones today with their unlimited communication abilities, we were bound by landlines that dialed out only to certain zip codes within a small radius before calls were considered long distance.

We made a plan to meet up at the party so we could kiss, but once we split off from everyone else, my courage and my plans dissolved before I could find the nerve to do it.

I wasn't the most skilled, romantically speaking, but I made up for it by honing a knack for basketball.

Once we moved to LaPoint, there were plenty of boys my age at church who I could play with. The church held tournaments for basketball, softball and coed volleyball. It didn't matter that my physical abilities were just above average to start–I now had teams to belong to and chances to get better at sports.

Eventually, I realized that playing sports exclusively in sweats was becoming not only embarrassing but excruciatingly hot. My parents wouldn't allow me to wear shorts—they believed it was immodest to show your legs, even for boys. Their distorted sense of modesty spanned all genders, so I resorted to the only option I had left: playing in jeans.

Most of my peers had the decency to ignore my ridiculous uniform. There were, however, plenty of them who laughed at me, pointing and jeering. Instead of hiding from that reality, I acted as if I wasn't mortified and simply told them the truth: "My parents don't allow me to wear shorts." It was hard for me to keep a straight face as I said it.

Jeff carved out a path to defy my parents, one small step at a time. He had no problem pushing them to their limits, especially when it came to music and TV.

One night, Jeff fell asleep before he remembered to turn off the radio in our room. Early the next morning, our father joined us at the table with a grave look of concern.

"Jeff, I woke up last night with the feeling that something was wrong in the house. I walked upstairs and heard a... *promiscuous* beat coming from your radio. I had to turn it off." My father's idea of provocative music was anything with a repetitive beat, a baseline or a fast tempo. In other words, anything that sounded like pop music must surely be a portal to hell, especially if he sensed a female singer was trying to seduce listeners with her voice.

Jeff stared back at my father flatly without blinking. "I like to fall asleep to the classical station at night," he explained, "but I've noticed lately they change their programming after midnight. That won't be happening again."

My brothers and I used to ride our bikes that we made from discarded parts at the county dump along the shoulder of the country highway near our home, collecting discarded aluminum cans to turn in at the recycling plant in Vernal. It was the only way we had to earn a few dollars, although it came with risks.

We stuck to the areas in front of farms and avoided venturing too close to the Ute settlements. Our father had made it clear that we were outsiders, and that message wasn't lost on us—or on the people whose land we bordered.

One afternoon, while scouring the sagebrush for cans, Ed spotted something unusual: a mangled cassette tape, clearly ejected from a car stereo and tossed out the window. Several feet of black tape had unraveled, fluttering like dark ribbon across the brush. Ed picked it up and wiped off the dust, squinting at the label. *Footloose: Original Motion Picture Soundtrack.*

We froze in disbelief. Though we'd heard some of the songs on our contraband radio, we couldn't believe our luck. Could we fix it somehow? Was this salvageable? Ed delicately gathered all the loose tape and tucked it carefully into his jacket pocket like he'd found buried treasure.

Just as we were about to move on, a truck pulled up slowly and stopped. A Native man inside leaned out the window, glaring. "What are you doing on our land?" he barked. Ed and Jeff quickly apologized, explaining we were just collecting cans.

The man said nothing at first. Then, slowly, he reached down by his door and raised his arm to show us the handgun he now held in his hand. He didn't aim it, but he didn't have to. "Get off our land," he said.

We jumped on our bikes like our lives depended on it—which, at that moment, they might have—and pedaled as fast as we could toward home. Behind us, the man laughed to himself, revved his engine and disappeared down the road.

We burst through the front door, breathless and rattled, terrified that our lives had just been threatened but relieved to be safe. Once the adrenaline wore off, Ed pulled the tape from his pocket and began the immediate work of restoration. The cassette was so badly damaged he had to open it entirely, unwind the entire reel by hand, splice the torn ribbon back together with Scotch tape and carefully rewind it using a pencil.

Somehow, against all odds, it worked. The tape played almost perfectly. There was just one loud scratch where the tape passed over the repaired splice. But it didn't matter, we had *Footloose*.

From that day on, it became the secret soundtrack of our lives. We only played it when we knew Dad was far enough away, likely tilling in the garden. We were tired of being hemmed in by the strict rules of overtly religious parents who viewed dancing and pop music as tools of the devil. We had risked danger to get that cassette, but the greater fear was still that our father would discover it. So we guarded it like a timeless relic and enjoyed it in secret.

The fact that it was *Footloose*—a story about teenagers fighting for the right to dance—was an irony too perfect to be accidental.

God must have a sense of humor.

The three of us were equally diligent when it came to our clandestine late night TV watching on dad's 12-inch black and white computer monitor for his Commodore 64. So together, we devised a plan with each of us in a defined role.

First, one of us would act as the lookout. Next, two of us could watch at a time. Third, the TV had to be concealed under a blanket to block the bright lights it emitted. Ideally, we'd keep the TV muted, but that defeated the purpose of watching music videos. We were to always remain vigilant, eyes and ears alert.

That black-and-white TV was our portal to the outside world. At the least, we had some things to talk about with regular kids. We studied the commercials that aired between videos as if we'd be tested on them afterward. We didn't know how to add or subtract, but at least we knew about G.I. Joe and McDonald's Happy Meals.

Our parents were none the wiser.

My father collected defunct cars with the sort of speed and aplomb one typically reserves for competitive spectator sports. He accumulated, then offloaded, dozens of vehicles as if they were trading cards. Of all the junkers he parked unceremoniously on our front lawn, his jewels were a half dozen of the Audi Fox. They became the Bagley mode of transport for two decades.

Dad trifled with cars of all shapes and sizes. We were most likely to find him hunched over a still-hot engine, playing the part of the temperamental mechanic, under some hood examining the guts of the motor a bit too closely.

He abided by one simple philosophy throughout our childhood: *keep two cars running, mine for specific parts from the others and buy brand new parts only under duress.* Breakdowns on the side of dirt roads became our family's singular tradition. I've lost track of how many vehicles I've helped push off the road to a narrow shoulder, melting at my increasing mortification each time.

Because of our proximity to multiple mountain ranges, we took regular trips to commune with nature. There was one occasion where my father outdid himself, this time in a shockingly positive way.

By the time there was nothing but empty road ahead and behind us, we started to notice the sure signs of our Audi overheating—not the least of which was a loud and halting death rattle floating up from the engine. Dad automatically unleashed a string of "*Goddamnits,*" swerving slightly each time his fist hit the dashboard. This was a Sunday, permitting me to smugly note his blasphemy on the Sabbath.

He pulled over on the side of the road, tiny pebbles crackling loudly beneath the tires. He wordlessly slammed the driver's side door shut, leaving us huddled together.

A note about seatbelts: this particular trip as a family happened in the 1980s, at a time when seatbelt laws were not as strict as they are today. Somehow, our entire family of 11 crammed into a four-door sedan. My father regularly thumbed his nose at the law, this time implicating the rest of us by outright discouraging us from using our seat belts. It was a small price to pay for a taste of freedom in the wilderness.

Somewhere hidden in this tinderbox of a car, he located the empty jug meant for radiator fluid. Like a surgeon with his scalpel, he propped open the hood to prepare for surgery.

Using his battered and oil-soaked signature red handkerchief as a filter, he gingerly filled the radiator with creek water he collected in a flurry of spastic movements. I hadn't spotted the water source, so I thought he might have some kind of sixth sense for finding hidden gems. He slammed the hood shut, jerking open the car door to get us on our way.

We barely made it two miles before billowing clouds of steam coughed up from the engine.

In his haste to deliver us from the evil of inconvenience, my father had forgotten the radiator cap somewhere along those desolate mountain miles.

His rage spilled over like magma with every fresh cloud that erupted before us. Dozens of F-bombs thundered from my father, further untethering me from the image of his piety. After what seemed like hours of fruitless backtracking along the blank roadside, Dad finally collapsed into sleep, leaving the rest of us motionless and puzzled, but not enough to speak up out of fear we might disrupt this fragile peace.

Once he awoke, Dad's expression shifted to stern concentration. He jumped out of the car, unsheathing the pocket knife he always kept razor-sharp. I followed his gaze to the quaking aspen trees dotting the mountains that surrounded us.

When I learned to read, I discovered that quaking aspen groves like these are considered the largest living organisms in the world. They have an extensive root system underground, an elaborate web of connective tissue.

As LDS members, we were always taught that humans were

meant to be *sealed* together in the afterlife to connect all of humanity for eternity. I saw these trees as symbols of that eternal joy, just beyond my reach. I wondered if God wanted me sealed to this family forever. I got lost in this thought, tracing and retracing the stark white bark and small circular leaves of each tree with my mind. If not for the leaves rustling as if they were chimes, I would not have known the wind was blowing.

Their movement gave me some small comfort that God was here, even when my parents failed to be.

After an even greater time, at least an hour or so more, my father emerged from the bank where he sat, presenting us with what looked to be a perfectly measured radiator cap he whittled from a tree's wood. He slowly and methodically twisted and untwisted the cap until it was secure. We observed his victory with the painful knowledge that if he had failed, we would have faced a nighttime trek maneuvering to ward off lurking mountain lions or Bigfoot encampments we were convinced existed.

The wooden cap held.

This handcrafted piece of aspen earned its place on our parents' dresser permanently. What I remember most about that trip was receiving the first sign that my father was more than what he wanted us to see. My mother clung to that cap for years, citing our father's ingenuity.

With his ingenious fix, I believe I saw my father to his core, if only for a moment.

That day, at least, he contained multitudes.

———

Dad bought an old Commodore 64 at Deseret Industries, the church-owned thrift store we called "the DI." He spent hours hunched over the tiny monitor, typing lines of code for some mysterious purpose. Eventually, I learned what it was: he had written a very simple program he believed could predict horse racing outcomes.

He claimed it wasn't gambling—it was investing. "If you know who's going to win," he told us at the kitchen table, "you're not gambling." Even as a child, I knew he was justifying.

He packed up the computer—and every dollar my parents had—and drove off to Las Vegas to test his system. I'd never even heard of Las Vegas before that. Jeff had to explain what and where it was.

The morning he left, Mom walked him out to the car as I trailed behind. She was visibly upset. He, on the other hand, was in the best mood I'd ever seen him in—grinning, joking, full of confidence. Just before getting in the car, he pulled Mom close and kissed her on the lips. It was the only time I ever saw them kiss. She smiled—briefly—then her face hardened. We waved as he drove away.

He was gone for more than three weeks. When he came back, the money was gone. The program had failed. He returned with nothing but a few photos of the Las Vegas LDS Temple under construction, as if the trip had been some kind of spiritual pilgrimage instead of a gambling spree.

But I knew the truth.

We were hungry at home, living under the threat of losing our house to repossession or the IRS. And while we struggled, my self-righteous, religious-zealot father was blowing what little money we had in the casinos of Las Vegas.

After Dad showed us the pictures, we never spoke of the trip again.

5. MORE FIT FOR THE KINGDOM

THE FIRST THING I NOTICED ABOUT OUR NEW HOME IN LAPOINT WAS the soil, its texture dense and rough, yet pliable. "No rocks," whispered Ben, as if to himself. I stood up slowly once I tested the earth for myself. My hands were still coated with freshly turned earth from digging in the potato cellar earlier that morning.

I nodded at Ben, wincing at the phantom weight of our dog Fritz that still lingered on my arms. I was the one who held Fritz as he drew his last breaths. We buried him next to the potato cellar behind the old shed, mainly to conceal the tears I was unable to prevent from slipping down my face.

Our new neighbor couldn't stand people, but he hated dogs more. One of our first mornings at the new house, our dad came running into the house shouting for me and Ben to come outside. We ran up to our father, hunched over Fritz. Our dog was fighting for his life.

Next to our convulsing dog, coughing up blood, we saw what looked like chewed-up and spat out raw hamburger meat. It didn't take long for us to figure out our neighbor's charm offensive: he had thrown poisoned meatballs over the fence for Fritz to find and ingest.

I swaddled our dying dog in my arms, frantically praying to God for help. I cried and cried. No help came. I feared this was the omen I didn't know I was expecting to see. I was neither surprised nor angry at what our loathsome neighbor had done. I should have anticipated *something* would scar our new life in LaPoint.

Wherever our family went, there we were.

And then, there were neighbors.

The walls of our new home seemed thin, exposed. Mom and Dad continued to shout at and over each other, but much less frequently. Whisper-fights became the norm. They knew we were no longer alone—the neighbors might hear.

Neighborhood kids pedaled past a couple of times while we were working in the front yard. "You guys coming to school tomorrow?" a freckled boy shouted.

"We'll see!" I lied, returning his wave while Ben chuckled beside me.

Our days were long and unenjoyable. From 8 a.m. to 3 p.m., Ben and I moved quietly around the house. Any pretense within the family that we were studying or learning was over. We all knew we didn't do schoolwork. Dad used to say all you needed to do was "teach a child to read and they will learn everything they need to know when they're ready."

We no longer needed the excuse of work to go outside to play. We struggled with how slowly the time passed otherwise. There are only so many cracks in the ceiling you can count before it grows old or you lose count. Our excitement returned whenever we heard the school bus rumbling by outside, our new neighbors chattering as they hopped off the bus.

LaPoint marked a change in our quality of life. I was now the oldest child at home and, with only five mouths to feed instead of eleven, things began to change. I started to notice little things at first when my mother unpacked groceries. All of a sudden, one grocery order included milk that we did not squeeze directly from a goat or store-bought bread and cheese. I nearly lost it when she pulled out a bag of generic Frosted Flakes. I did my best to appear casual, like I hadn't noticed my mother's 180-degree turn from extremism to some kind of secularist compromise.

Most of the boys my age in LaPoint seemed far too cool for my company. I'm not convinced I had a full grasp of what *cool* entailed, but I knew enough to know I was not it. Regardless, those boys were all much kinder to me than they needed to be. Once I turned 14, I hit a growth spurt—thankfully Jeff left me some bigger clothes when he moved away.

I had one clean pair of jeans I was willing to wear in public, but they were much too short for my lanky frame. Those high-waters only got higher as I grew. My solution—wearing long tube socks I hoped might fill in the gap—lasted a couple of years.

I tried to own the fact that I might as well have been an extraterrestrial passing as a human; I was uncomfortable to say the least. I remember one guy laughing when he saw my pants, but otherwise the memory doesn't sting like others have before it.

We spent a fair amount of time with the kids in the Bascom family who lived close by. They had teenagers who were fun to be around, especially Garth, who was a little older than me. Garth took an interest in my homeschool situation and was someone I could confide in. I told him I hated it, but my parents made me do it. He said, "that sucks." Then we went about living our lives. More importantly, it didn't change that we were friends. It didn't change the way he saw me like it did with most kids my age.

I started sneaking out of the house Friday and Saturday nights to hang out with him and my budding group of friends. One night, I snuck out of the house especially late, escaping through my window. I came back after midnight from playing kick-the-can in the park with a mixed group of teenagers, boys and girls. I tiptoed through the yard and started to squeeze through my bedroom window when I heard my father's voice.

"Did you have a good time?"

I froze, uncertain if he expected me to respond.

"What were you doing tonight?" he asked, curiosity more than anger creeping in his tone.

I gave him the basic information, still anxious to head off an explosion—if it wasn't already too late.

"Well, you better get to bed. It's late."

I detected nothing but calm and concern in his voice. I shook my head and slowly made my way to the door. He never mentioned that night again.

———

I couldn't wait to turn 12 years old, because that meant I was eligible for Boy Scout camp. Scout camp was the one exception to our parents never allowing us to leave their side. I remember when my older brothers would spend weeks at camp each summer, and I spent that time dreaming of all the things I would do once it was my turn.

I was still considered a Lone Scout, but my father was able to arrange for me to join a troop from Neola, Utah. Being a Lone Scout meant that I was sort of a self-study in the wilderness arts, but now I could become a part of a real community. I especially dominated at the knot-tying competitions. Praise from the Scoutmaster and fellow Scouts earned me the prize of one bag of classic M&M's.

I accepted the bag as if I had been handed a brick of gold. I ogled it, knowing my parents would not approve. Without hesitating, I ripped open the bag and put the first piece of chocolate I'd ever tasted in my mouth. It was sweet and decadent, made more so by the fact that no one could take this experience away from me. I did not make any attempts to slow myself down, so I demolished the entire bag in a couple of bites. Once I tasted chocolate, I couldn't stop thinking about it.

Nothing could be better.

———

I marveled at the majesty of the mountain lake rippling before me, its body reflecting a cloudless sky. The water was so clear I could see smooth stones at the bottom. The air smelled of pine and bug spray. The voices of boys laughing and splashing in the water echoed off the granite peaks surrounding our camp.

I alternated feet, stepping gently onto the rocky shore, the loose stones making standing difficult for too long a time. The water met my toes every few seconds with its ebb and flow of shocking cold, daring me to come closer. Still, I slowly waded forward.

"You can do it! You got this!" Danny shouted from the wooden dock across the water. I closed my eyes to hear the sound of water gently lapping against the red canoe that bobbed beside him, its aluminum paddle popping in and out of the water.

The other boys didn't seem to have any issues completing their swim tests. They made it all look so effortless: confident strokes, arms cutting through the water with ease. I had watched them closely and hoped to mimic their movements because I held a secret. I didn't know how to swim and had never been in water above my head.

The buoy speckled with dirt floated about thirty yards out from shore, just a bright orange dot that might as well have been the moon. I sucked in the fresh air, my arms held in position above the water as if to tame a violent sea.

First, the water covered my ankles. Then, my knees were completely submerged. I felt my bathing suit soak in the freezing cold water just in time to remind me I should have used the bathroom before I started.

Once I had waded out waist-deep, I felt the gradual descent of the sandy bottom sloping downward. I took a gulp and launched myself forward, my arms shooting out in front of me like a civilian saluting soldiers. I had imagined mimicking the skilled and liquid movements of the other boys, but mine were closer to the thrashing motions of a wounded animal. I panicked, my arms windmilling frantically to try to stop the water from consuming me whole. I lost energy quickly as I struggled to keep my head above water. My mouth and nose protested in vain against the brackish water spilling over my face. My feet no longer touched the bottom of the lake.

I hadn't planned on being a casualty that day, especially not with witnesses looking on just 20 feet from shore.

"Grab the paddle!" A boy in the canoe, now in motion, thrust an aluminum blade toward me to grab. I fumbled until my fingers locked around the lifeline. The boy paddled with one oar slowly through the water back to shore with my limp body in tow.

Once we reached the shore, I collapsed while still gasping for air. I coughed and coughed while lake water streamed from my nose. My body shook from cold, embarrassment, shame and the terrifying realization I had almost drowned.

———

I approached the empty check-in station nervous but excited. My friends and I dropped our duffel bags by our feet like abandoned cargo, ready to settle into what promised to be the adventure of a lifetime. The camp leader absently scratched his head, examining the clipboard in his hand without ever looking up at us.

"Go ahead and take the trail that goes past the amphitheater," he said while waving us through. "There's an overflow site back there. We can figure out your site assignments later."

We followed the trail, which wound through a dense forest. The path was worn from the boots of previous campers, and the ground surrounding us was like a giant carpet made of pine needles. I recognized a couple of distinct bird calls from perches high above us.

If I had to name the happiest place on earth, here at Boy Scout camp would be it.

The overflow campsite was filled with excited campers. We stood around our small clearing in the woods, complete with a fire pit and smooth tree stubs for seating. Our group looked at each other with smug grins, dropping our gear to explore our surroundings.

"Did anyone actually see us walk back here?" asked Jake, the oldest boy in our group.

For six glorious days, our little sequestered spot in the woods and our apparent anonymity gave us freedom that other campers did not enjoy. We were like feudal lords overseeing the comings and goings of our plot of land. We'd lazily roll out of our sleeping bags once the sun appeared high enough in the sky to cast its warming light on our faces. Breakfast was served for the entire camp at the mess tent. I loaded my tray with a hearty breakfast of scrambled eggs, bacon (a meat my parents believed to be unclean) and hash browns piled into a delicious heap.

Nobody asked for our names once or checked any list to confirm our arrival.

We played Capture the Flag, whittled small pieces of wood by the fire pit and engaged in long conversations while looking for streams in the forest. When we heard the dinner bell ring, we'd emerge undetected with the crowd of hundreds of scouts milling into the mess tent.

At nightfall, our voices dropped to baritone range as we mingled around the fire. We took turns hurling different objects into the flames, testing their intensity and willingness to grow. We stayed up for hours past the campwide call for lights out, talking well into the wee hours of the morning.

In the rare moments of silence, we could hear owls hooting overhead. As I lay my head down for the night, the smell of campfire smoke emanated from my clothing.

I didn't mind at all.

———

The eastern rim of Flaming Gorge looked as brilliantly lit as an atomic blast, the morning sun erupting over its rockface. The red sandstone cliffs boasted shades of copper and gold, and the high desert air wore thin at 6,200 feet. Nature provided no protection for the kind of solar radiation breaking through the atmosphere.

At this great height—with our nearing proximity to the sky—the sun was lethal.

I was eager to bare my skin, but particularly my legs, by wearing swim trunks. According to my parents, shorts were immodest and forbidden, even for boys. My 15 year-old virgin skin was so white it was almost translucent. Even I was shocked by my lack of skin tone; my limbs looked like the underbelly of a jellyfish. I spent the entirety of my childhood ruefully untouched by the sun and I was ready to be free.

We reached a reservoir filled entirely with liquid sapphire. I touched the water hesitantly, the memory of my woeful swim test still fresh and a bit too close to the surface. The water was unusually cold, especially with the snowmelt that trickled down from the mountain peaks. The chill of the water made me gasp, my skin instantly covered in goosebumps.

I chose an inner tube as my floating confidence, drifting slowly into the water as my friends dove and splashed with abandon. I became aware, at least unconsciously, that being out on the water exposed us to the cloudless sky for long stretches of time. After two hours, the skin on my shoulders and chest felt agitated. Once three hours on the water floated by, the heat began to feel like a living organism poking and prodding me as it crawled across my back.

Noon came and went. I had convinced myself that dangling my legs in the cool mountain water would regulate the temperature for me. I convinced myself that this was all orchestrated for me to live my best life. Except my skin began to tingle with warmth, followed by a somewhat unpleasant full-body flush.

By 2 p.m., the tingling became a low-grade burning sensation. But still, I could not be bothered to move from my rightful place atop the inner tube. I would not be the first to surrender to the sun.

As 3 p.m. arrived, my skin felt stretched tight like a snare drum. The entire surface area of my body ached.

An hour later, the time of judgment drew near. My skin, now as brittle and delicate as air-dried crepe paper soaked by a spill, felt like it had been set on fire.

I made the mistake of peeking down at my legs, which were now so red they appeared purple. Every inadvertent brush of clothing or even air on my skin felt like an assault.

"Maybe we should head back," one of my friends suggested. He sounded far away, but close enough that I listened. When my legs hit the surface of the water, I suppressed a scream. Despite the near-frozen chill of the water, I felt as if my legs were eternal flames that could not be extinguished. When my friends caught a glimpse of my charred remains, they stopped in mid-sentence.

Every movement was agonizing. The short walk back to camp felt more like the twisting steps leading downward into layers of Dante's Inferno. I managed to put my clothing back on, a choice that only seemed to intensify my pain. My scout pants might as well have been chainmail grating hotly against my throbbing skin. By the time we reached camp, I looked like an overripe tomato forgotten in the late summer sun.

During dinner, I tried to pretend everything was normal and not deep-fried. I ate beans and cornbread as casually as I could. Meanwhile, I winced at even the smallest movement of my hand lifting the fork to my mouth. I was terrified that I had done real and lasting damage to my body with a burn this severe.

I had only just begun to understand the full scope of disaster I had brought upon myself.

When I stood to leave the mess tent, the muscles in my legs seized involuntarily. It took me at least double the time it normally would have to make my way from the mess tent to our campsite. Once I sat down on a wooden stump by the fire, I tried to gently take off my pants to change into something with less material. I couldn't get them off. The fabric seemed to have fused to my skin that was now swollen with heat as boils began filling in my second-degree burns.

I tried hard to stop myself from hyperventilating. I was completely thrown when my body began producing cold, sharp panic jolts radiating from within. This wasn't just a sunburn; it was something like sun poisoning that required treatment I couldn't access here in the desert. Dusk set in quickly when I realized my father was a mile away having his own experience as a scout leader, unaware that his son was cooked from the inside out.

I made the fateful decision to seek his help.

The dirt road leading to his campsite looked like an endless rope to climb, all while trying to beat nightfall. My flashlight beam dimmed then began to flash intermittently like a strobe light. Every step I took down the road refreshed my agony. The pants I was unable to remove rubbed against my skin like steel wool and each step made me sweat profusely.

The distant lights from the Jamboree, the temporary city Boy Scout campers erected, gave me a semblance of hope. I moved slowly as I passed empty tents along the perimeter, working my way through new voices that carried music and overlapping conversations.

Then, all at once, the darkness overtook me. I could no longer make out tents in the dark, not even their outlines. I couldn't see fires or hear voices anymore, either. I didn't realize how far I had walked beyond our tent city.

The desert looked empty in the darkness that engulfed me.

I stopped walking for a moment to catch my breath. Panic

clawed at my chest when I admitted to myself I could not find Dad's campsite in the dark. Where had I made a wrong turn?

Suddenly, bright white beams bobbed in the distance. I felt overcome with relief and gratitude.

Thank you! I thought to God and no one. *Someone can help me.*

"Hey!" I called out too eagerly. "Can you help me find my dad?" I had no idea who may have heard me—I still couldn't see more than a few paces ahead of me in the dark. The lights stopped bobbing and shifted toward the ground. One shone directly in my face. I shielded my eyes against the glare, raising my hand to block the light.

"Who are you?" A disembodied voice spoke in the darkness.

"I'm Calvin Bagley," I stammered, painfully aware of how lost and young and scared I sounded. "I'm on staff. I'm trying to find my dad."

Lights quickly separated, then reunited to encircle me. I still could not make out anyone's figure, let alone their face. My stomach dropped to see I was surrounded by random strangers who didn't seem interested in being Good Samaritans.

"I'm trying to find my *daddy*," one of them mocked me with a saccharine-sweet voice.

Others in what sounded like a small crowd continued the chant: "*Find my daddy...find my daddy...*" I looked everywhere and nowhere to see who I was up against. I tried to feign laughter in the dark, but my voice cracked unconvincingly. I sensed the circle tighten around me, my eyes adjusting to what seemed like shadows of figures shifting.

The first blow landed against my back with a loud *thwack*.

For a split second, I believed that the unremitting pain I felt was caused by a towel whipping at my sunburn in jest. Then I felt the ensuing explosion of agony that lit up my nervous system with alarming severity.

They all began to hit me with cacti.

Hundreds of needles pierced through my shirt, ripping into my sunburn simultaneously. I felt my body topple to the ground.

I instinctively rolled myself into a ball to ward off the constant blows raining down on me.

In the arc of one arm elevated to strike, I caught a glimpse of their chosen weapons: long sticks with clusters of Eve's Needle cactus spines fastened as "crackers" or "poppers" at the ends.

I'm not sure how long they sustained the attack—or why.

I felt needles drive deeper and deeper into my back, my legs and my arms. I tasted blood in my mouth mixed with salt from the tears falling down my face.

And then, as suddenly as the attack began, it stopped.

I was coiled on the ground nursing my wounds when I noticed the lights retreat into darkness. Their voices laughed and whooped in the distance while I held onto consciousness with a tentative grip.

I lay there in the dirt, sobbing and shaking. I shuddered when I considered that even scout camp was not a place where I knew I was safe or deserving of peace.

The heavy night sky watched this cruelty unfold, answering with only blinking stars and nebulous constellations.

———

The Professional Scouter fixed his propane lantern beside me, its harsh white light calling attention to the horror covering me. The staffer bent over me with tweezers that he struggled to steady with his shaky hands. His face was pinched with sympathy but also anger at what had happened to me.

"This is going to hurt," he mumbled, though we both knew there wasn't much worse than what I had already endured.

I lay with my face down on the picnic table, biting the sleeve of my shirt as if it were a leather strap. Each time he tweezed a needle from my skin, it felt like I was being stabbed repeatedly. The warm trickle of blood down my sides was the only evidence I had that I had not succumbed to the pain or death. He placed each needle on the table beside my head so that I could see precisely what those monsters had done to me.

Staff gathered around the table, trying to make sense of what had occurred. There were words of fury and confusion while people asked, "Who would do this?" I had no answers and the perpetrators left no clues, besides the needles drawn from my back.

Eventually, after a painfully long wait, my father finally arrived at the campsite. The Professional Scouter's voice was tight with anger as he explained what had happened. He hardly attempted to conceal his rage while explaining the situation to my father. "You need to take him to the hospital. Now."

My father began to protest with his body language, something I was now accustomed to reading before he spoke. I knew his arguments by heart—high hospital bills, the long drive out to the facility, the untrustworthy doctors—and I anticipated every last one. Instead, one glare from the Professional Scouter asserted that a visit to the hospital was not optional.

My father pretended to concede the point, though it became clear almost immediately as we drove away that we were headed for our house not to the hospital. It mattered very little to me. I did not think I could heal from pain this immense, whether I was convalescing at an emergency room or in my bedroom.

I pressed my face against the cool car window, anticipating the sweet relief of sleep or death.

My mom looked shaken at the sight of me walking through the door. Her face may have even registered concern, though I had no point of reference. My clothes were stiffened and bloodied, a sight that somehow dimmed in comparison to my skin, which was wickedly scorched with severe sunburns and boils. She drew an ice-cold bath for me without asking, and I lowered myself into the tub without complaint. I shivered through the freezing bath to numb the pain from the needles, though the cold felt unbearable on my skin.

For weeks afterward, I couldn't sleep on my back. The skin

on my legs peeled first, divesting from my body like a molting snake. But my back took the longest to heal. I still resembled a pincushion months after the attack.

I don't know what led those teenage boys to do something so brutal; maybe the cruelty was the point. But my desire to further attend scout camps was extinguished that day.

I had learned a difficult lesson that monsters don't always look like monsters. Sometimes they wear uniforms, say prayers and sleep in tents next to yours.

———

My world had expanded from LaPoint to Roosevelt, from scout camps to coed dances, with two constants: Brian and Garth.

I continued to pass myself off as normal, going so far as to pursue my driver's education class in the hallowed halls of Uintah High School, Room 201. I remember the first night of class, arriving way too early just to linger in the halls by myself trying to look busy. I was nervous—this was the first time I had ever been inside a school before. I peered through the windows of the classrooms marveling at what was inside. As I walked closer to the only lit classroom, I heard voices spill into the hall-way. I faked confidence unconvincingly, walking into the room just as the record seemed to stop.

Thirty strange teenagers turned to look at me all at once. I spotted an empty seat and walked toward it.

"Hey, Doogie Howser! Is that really you?" someone called out. Dr. Howser was a precocious teen TV doctor played by Neil Patrick Harris of *How I Met Your Mother* and Broadway fame. He was a mega famous child actor in the 1990s.

Everyone laughed, but not at my expense. Our instructor, Mr. Blackburn, smiled to himself while checking his atten-dance sheet.

"Well, I'll be. You look just like him," he said, simultaneously checking off my name. "Please take your seat, Dr. Howser."

My parents never cared much for Halloween, but I knew it was time for me to jump into the scene if only to show I knew *something* about pop culture.

I reasoned that it would be a missed opportunity if I didn't dress the part—I *became* Doogie.

I styled my hair like Neil Patrick Harris—so precisely, in fact, that I parted my hair on the opposite side to match his. I scrounged the bins at thrift stores to find a stethoscope, a lab coat and a prop ID badge. My costume was a wild success. The neighbors who rang our doorbell that night gasped when I answered the door. "The resemblance is uncanny," the Petersons, our neighbors across the street, observed.

At the risk of seeming painfully lame, I must admit that my resemblance to Doogie Howser positioned me as someone I'd always wanted to be: a normal kid, but exceptional. This was the first time in my life I was known for something other than being homeschooled.

The irony, of course, was brutal: I was a homeschooled kid with no education, pretending to be a teenage doctor who'd already graduated from medical school. I couldn't even do my times tables, but for one night, I was going to be Doogie.

By Christmas, I'd earned "Doogie" as my permanent nickname.

———

Bishop Huber stands at the pulpit for a youth and parent fireside dispatching advice while my mind sets adrift with daydreams.

"Remember, the standards from The Strength of the Youth pamphlet," he continues, scanning the congregation until his gaze finally settles on me. "Proper dating begins at 16, and not a day before."

As if I could forget.

I feel my mother's grip on my knee, her fingernails leaving

half-moon crescents dented in my skin. My father nods in agreement, a bit too enthusiastically for my liking.

Two weeks pass, and Bishop Huber's son, Blaine, corners me
once we close out the service in prayer.

"My girlfriend has a friend she wants to bring to the bonfire
on Saturday," he whispers. My muscles tense and my skin grows
cold and clammy. I gulp. "Oh, cool. What's her name?"
I stammer.

"Laura," he says, leaning in closer, "and she's really cute."

With his urgent message delivered, Blaine adjusts his tie
while I contemplate the situation. Blaine is two years older than
me and preparing to leave on his mission. "How old is Laura?" I
ask while acting nonchalant with Blaine.

"I kind of need you to come. My dad says I have to double-
date until after my mission. You in?"

He had me at "bonfire."

That Saturday night, my mother insists on gifting me with a
crisp 20-dollar bill. She presses it in my palm firmly, as if to
grease it with some corrupting bribe.

"This is how it should be," she opines, speaking to no one
in particular.

I watch her eyes wander over the framed family photos on
our wall, zeroing in on Jeff's face. She shoos away the potted
plant's leaves obscuring her view.

"I'll pay for your dates if you promise not to get a job." Our
mother believes it was Jeff's job that corrupted him. She would
rather finance my date night than take the chance of me
becoming self-sufficient.

Blaine's Oldsmobile idles outside in our driveway, beckoning
to me like a siren's song. His girlfriend, Suzie, is already waiting
patiently on the porch for me to greet her. Behind her, half-
hidden by dusk's shadows, stands a girl with straight, sleek
chestnut-colored hair spilling over her shoulders.

So this must be Laura.

We take our places in the back seat, cautiously sizing each

other up. Our eyes meet in the rearview mirror before I quickly look away.

The bonfire comes and goes without incident, both Laura and I are too shy to make much conversation.

Laura and I sit next to each other, moving with hardly any effort. The metal swings creak beneath us, our toes dragging through the sand every so often. Our hands are intertwined like a lattice.

Roosevelt City Park at dusk is a lush canvas of our lengthening shadows on manicured lawns. We hear Blaine and Suzie giggling quietly on the merry-go-round, forgetting entirely that we are here, too.

"Quick, before they look," she whispers as she leans close enough that I can feel her breath on my face.

My pulse jumps and my heart palpitates against my ribs. I close my eyes prematurely, bumping my nose against hers. She forgives my clumsiness by lifting her lips up to mine, touching hers tightly to mine for a moment.

I pull away, unsure of what to do with myself next. I feel as if I've just witnessed this scene from above, looking down at my own inexperience endearing me to her. I feel my face grow hotter as I try to slow my breath. I am still floating, and I don't know if I'll ever come down.

"Was that your first kiss?" she asks, squeezing my hand tighter.

I nod, sure of my crimson flush by now.

"Don't worry," she said with a smile. "We'll practice."

Kissing practice becomes my favorite activity. We find every darkened corner of every church parking lot within a 30-mile radius. We pay for empty rows at the Roosevelt Cinema, forgetting to watch countless movies. Laura teaches me what to do with my hands without pushing things too far. I don't stop to think that maybe this is supposed to mean something.

One frigid winter night, Laura asks me something I have not prepared for.

"I was talking to Suzie and she told me she's going to wait for Blaine when he goes on his mission in the spring."

Oh. So that's how this happens. I think I know where this is going.

"When you go on your mission..." She hesitates. "I could wait, too. For you."

Her expectant eyes search mine for confirmation. My stomach clenches into knots. What she is proposing is a near-impossibility. She's getting ready to go to college, but I just turned 16. Three years until I turn 19, then two years on my mission—five years loom over me like a cloud threatening rain. I am not ready to devote any of my youthful independence to one single girl, let alone five years. I know so many of my peers are eager to get married, especially because most of us are saving our virginity for our future wives. But I know I can't make this commitment to her.

"Laura, I..."

No words come to rescue me.

We meet again, two nights later. We embrace each other on her porch, our breath creating small clouds in the frigid air.

She drops her head to avoid seeing my reaction. "I just don't get it. What changed?"

Nothing I say satisfies her. I repeat the only thing I know to say or to feel: "I'm sorry. I'm so sorry."

"You act like I dreamed us up in my head—it's as if you weren't really here with me all along." She holds back her tears, attempting to regain her composure.

Her eyes meet mine one last time. She no longer looks at me with a loving gaze; her eyes now look upon me with pity.

"I hope you find what you're looking for." She kisses my cheek, then spins her heel to walk inside.

If only I knew.

———

My first glimpses of freedom were nothing compared to the elation I felt when I visited Jeff in Las Vegas for the first time. He had just divorced Crystal—at exactly the same time Belinda's marriage to Joe unraveled, and not by coincidence. Joe had traveled to Las Vegas to offer one of his signature therapeutic hypnosis sessions. What happened instead was something else entirely. The real story is perhaps too salacious for print, but my siblings had lost their spouses in the same week.

Las Vegas assaulted my senses with its neon signs and smoke-filled casinos. Vegas was a galaxy apart from LaPoint's dusty antiquity, and Jeff's life looked like pure freedom to me. He filled his refrigerator with whatever he wanted. He came and went without answering to anyone.

He saw how spellbound I was. "You could have this, too," he told me one night. "You're almost 18." I looked over the balcony at the city lights below, amazed at how easy it was to agree with him. "Yeah, I know," I sighed.

I came home from that visit a changed person. My mother could sense it—I could tell by her deeply suspicious tone.

"I want a job," I said through clenched teeth.

"You know my answer to that," she replied, eyeing my father to back her up. He nodded without looking up from his manuscript.

"Jeff said I'll have a place to stay if I need it. I can pay rent. I can be independent."

My mother's face fell when I mentioned Jeff. He had, in her mind, abandoned her and the family with his departure. She had screamed and cried. And there sat Crystal, arms firmly crossed at her chest, waiting in an idling car for Jeff to collect his things.

"You wouldn't dare," she whispered, half threatening, half pleading. "You won't, will you?"

I allowed her question to hang in the air.

I had already made my decision. Having tasted real freedom, I discovered something I knew I needed to have. It was only a question of when.

In short order, I started earning my own money and bought a car. The more I relied on myself, the less I looked to my parents for approval. They wanted me home by midnight on weekends, but I could not—would not—abide. I had already begun the planning for my mission, a spiritual adventure I disinvited them to the moment I committed to going.

Despite my defiance, I was never able to fully forget how frightening my mom had always been. Part of what motivated me was my desire to assert my independence, but also to experience life without being under her thumb. For once, I needed to breathe in the absence of ever-present danger.

I managed to save $2,500 for my mission, enough to cover the cost of all the suits and clothes I had to buy. My mom promised to pay for the rest. I worked with my bishop to prepare all of the paperwork to submit to Salt Lake City. A few weeks after my 19th birthday, the letter I'd waited to receive my entire life finally arrived. I held my breath as I tore open the envelope.

The first words I read made me dizzy with overwhelming glee.

"Dear Elder Bagley, You are hereby called to serve as a missionary of The Church of Jesus Christ of Latter-day Saints. You have been recommended as one worthy to represent the Lord as a minister of the restored gospel. You are assigned to labor in the Brazil Curitiba Mission."

I exhaled all of the contents in my lungs, immediately drinking in gulps of new air as my adrenaline started pumping. My next thought startled me: Where on Earth, is Brazil? I'd never even studied a proper map, let alone a globe.

"Is that in Africa?" I wondered aloud.

———

Preparation for my mission began almost instantly. I had six weeks to purchase everything I didn't have, from clothing and shoes to luggage and toiletries.

It was autumn when my parents drove me to the Missionary Training Center (MTC) in Provo, Utah to drop me off for the first leg of my trip. My mother cried. My father told me he was happy with my decision. I no longer expected either of them to figure out how to tell me they were proud of me—I didn't need them to.

My father often cited a General Conference talk by President Ezra Taft Benson to justify never showing pride in me or any of his children. In his mind, pride was showing enmity toward God, so there couldn't be such a thing as righteous pride. I suspect my father loved that speech because it fooled him into thinking his lack of ambition and success was due to humility rather than character flaws. His self-soothing no longer mattered to me; I was proud of how far I had come and for what I accomplished just by making it this far.

The MTC included a two-month immersive language-training program. I lived in a dorm room with three other missionaries. As burgeoning missionaries, boys were called "elder" and girls were called "sister." For the next two years, I would be known as Elder Bagley.

My companion, Elder Deitz, joined me for companionship scripture study time at 7 a.m. every morning, followed by breakfast and language classes and concluding with devotionals.

Sundays became special in a new way. We attended church together, then gathered in a large hall to hear from prominent church leaders visiting from nearby Salt Lake City. One day a week was our Preparation Day or P-day for short. We followed that schedule each and every day. The further along we were in our studies, the happier and more excited I became.

I was baffled by how many of the missionaries in my group expressed homesickness or longing for their girlfriends. They noticed my unbridled joy, joking that "We are all missing home, but Bagley thinks he's at Disneyland!" They had a point.

The only thing I missed was my car.

6. "VALEU A PENA"

I SWEAR I CAN HEAR MY HEARTBEAT OVER THE SOUND OF THE BUS'S engine as we pull up to Salt Lake City International Airport. I spot my father's head bobbing first, Uvene and Ben hand-in-hand next to him.

My dad greets me with a giant bear hug. I do not know whether to hug him back.

We settle into the hard plastic chairs close to my gate. Dad takes out his pocket knife and sharpening stone and begins sharpening his blade. As swishing sounds echo through the terminal, I squirm under the collective judgment of a dozen raised eyebrows. Announcements crackle over the loudspeaker: delays to Denver, to Chicago. None for Atlanta. I pray for a speedy departure.

"Nice tie, dork," Ben teases. I wish I could bring him with me. More for his sake than mine. Uvene shines a bright smile in my direction, warming my heart more than I expect it to.

I take advantage of our early arrival, thumbing through my Portuguese phrasebook, re-reading the pages already dog-eared from my time at the MTC. "Bom dia. Como vai você?" I mutter. I repeat this phrase and others to myself.

I drum my fingers anxiously against my knee, checking the clock for the 50th time in 15 minutes.

"Final boarding call for flight 847 to Atlanta."

My father sheaths his knife and sharpening stone, then clears his throat, barely reaching above a whisper. "You are going there for God. Remember who you are—remember who *we* are."

There he is, I think. He can't help himself.

But none of that matters anymore.

I hoist my carry-on over my left shoulder, nearly flipping myself onto my back like a *tartaruga*—a turtle.

The plane is stuffy and smells of body odor—and it's glorious. Elder Deitz nudges me as we settle into our coach seats. "You okay, man? You look a little green around the gills."

I smile and nod to humor him. I grip the armrests as the plane takes off, mouthing verb conjugations under my breath. "Eu sou, você é, ele é..." becomes my liftoff prayer.

When we touch down in Atlanta, the missionaries finally splinter off to their respective gates. Elders are heading to Belo Horizonte, to Salvador, to Rio. All at once, my companion and I are the two remaining missionaries at Gate C42.

The next leg of our trip happens quickly. When we board the Varig Brazil plane, a haze of stale smoke hits me. A flight attendant with ruby lips ushers us forward, motioning with two manicured fingers. "Non-smoking, sim?"

I scan the rows of passengers just as a wispy curtain ripples ahead, revealing dozens more rows—passengers chatting, some already lighting cigarettes.

"So much for non-smoking," Elder Deitz bemoans.

I find our seats without any trouble, angling for the window. When I collapse into my seat, I welcome the air streaming from the tiny vent above me.

Daylight cedes to dusk without me noticing. I sleep in fits and starts, punctuated only by my waking bursts of coughing fits whenever multiple passengers click their lighters. I scribble a note to myself in Portuguese: "Lava esta camisa." (This trans-lates to "wash this shirt.")

I gasp when the plane draws close enough to see the glit-tering maze of concrete and streetlights of São Paulo. The city looks big enough to fit ten cities in one.

We move slowly through customs behind a man chirping angrily in rapid Portuguese at stone-faced officials. I clutch my passport with white knuckles, fumbling to hand it to a grumpy customs officer.

"Propósito da visita?" the agent asks without looking up.

"Sou...um missionário." My words sound garbled and disjointed.

He stamps my passport then waves me through anyway. I passed my first test. With that, we make our way through the São Paulo airport to our connecting flight.

———

Deitz and I pat ourselves on the back for arriving mere moments before looking around the Curitiba airport to see not a single welcome sign or friendly face. There is nothing familiar about this place at all.

Our wait becomes an hours-long saga. "Maybe they forgot about us," Deitz says, unbuttoning his collared shirt.

I spot some kind of officer and try to ask him anything that could get me an answer as to who is meant to meet us here.

"Ficha," he repeats, pointing at the phone. "Ficha!"

My brain can't work fast enough to translate. My face burns, sweat trickling down my back. "Desculpe, não entendo." "I'm so sorry," I cry, "I don't understand."

The man's face melts into a soft expression as he digs into his pocket. He hands me a small metal token meant for the phone. "Ficha," he says softly, as if to a child.

"Ficha," I repeat, still trying to make sense of the shape my mouth forms when I say it. "Obrigado! Muito obrigado!" I thank him profusely.

I dial the mission office on the phone, "Missão Curitiba, como posso ajudar?" comes the voice on the line. I attempt to answer him with what I think will suffice: my name and my destination.

He hears my accent and abruptly switches to English. "Hold up, you're American? Aren't you supposed to arrive tomorrow?"

I sigh with relief, despite the obvious setback. We figure out the logistics then Elder Deitz and I wait for their arrival.

I start to nod off a bit while sitting up until I spot a dust-covered sedan pull up outside of the terminal. A clean-cut missionary with a sunburned neck jumps out to greet us.

"Welcome to Brazil, Elders! President Damiani is waiting for you."

———

Steel elevator doors slide open to reveal polished hardwood floors and the aroma of simmering feijões and garlic. President Damiani, a slender man with salt-and-pepper hair, extends his hand.

"Bem-vindo ao Brasil, Elders," he says, guiding us into a spacious living room with floor-to-ceiling windows that frame Curitiba's skyline.

Sister Damiani joins us from the kitchen, wiping her hands on a cloth. "Thirteen floors up," she says with a wink. Her eyes drift upward. "Only we wanted this place. Brazilians won't live on the 13th floor anywhere. They say it's bad luck."

Dinner is exciting and entertaining. The children pepper us with questions, one after the other. We devour feijoada that makes my tongue tingle with unfamiliar spices and infinite possibilities. President Damiani's wedding ring clinks against his water glass, calling even the children's attention to him.

"Elder Deitz," he says, "you'll be staying here in Curitiba with Elder Cardoso." I sit in awe, slack-jawed. "Elder Bagley, tomorrow you'll travel to Ponta Grossa. Elder Mouhamed will be waiting for you there."

My spoon freezes midway to my mouth. "Ponta Grossa?" (*What? Where? How?*)

"The mountains are breathtaking. You'll love it," Sister Damiani assures me, patting my arm.

I excuse myself from dinner. Splashing water on my face extinguishes the panic emanating from my every pore.

"Ponta Grossa," I say to myself dreamily, until I fall asleep. My new mantra.

The morning greets me with a rush of diesel fumes and vendors shouting indiscriminately at the rodoviária. I'm flanked by two assistants in oxford shirts, whisking me and my luggage away in record time.

"Your bus leaves in twenty minutes, Elder," the taller assistant explains while guiding me through a thick crowd of families and chickens scuttling underfoot. "Bus seven is yours. The ride should take an hour and a half."

I settle into a vinyl seat that's seen some life. Leaning my forehead against the window, I notice a cluster of fingerprints smudged on the glass and it makes me smile. I immediately fall in love with scenes along my route—women balancing baskets on their heads, teenagers staring out of windows, elders of a different sort playing cards on upturned crates.

And then I see them.

A young man no older than 25, wearing a faded blue t-shirt bright against his deeply tanned skin, crouches down to be eye-level with a toddler whose tiny fist curls around the man's extended pointer finger. The little one looks upward with absolute trust. The man says something playfully, and the boy's laughter bubbles up, high and clear over the chaos.

Before I know it, my eyes are misty. I think this might be the ice thawing; it's what has encased my heart for as long as I can remember. Something else shifts within me, imperceptible almost: I realize I want what I've just seen—I want to be a father.

My chest tightens as I watch the pair disappear into the crowd, the boy's chubby legs walking double time to keep up with his dad's.

That kind of love exists within me—improbably—not at all dimmed by time or chronic heartbreak.

And it's mine to give.

The bus heaves forward with an uproar of black smoke behind us. I stare absently through the window at the same space where the father and son stood moments before, unaware of the dozens of people now crowded there.

Requited love, I think. That must be it.

The landscape transforms from a sparkling city to rolling hills, mountains stacked against each other.

Yet, amid all this beauty, the only thing I see is a son whose tiny hand is wrapped around his father's finger.

"Elder Bagley!" A cheerful voice calls from across the Ponta Grossa station platform. A lean and lithe Brazilian man with dark eyes and a sharply angled jawline waves me over.

"Elder Mouhamed," I say, extending my hand eagerly. "Prazer em conhecê-lo."

He nods buoyantly, taking my heaviest bag off my hands. "Your Portuguese is not so bad."

I answer in English with a big smile. "Do you speak any En—"

He cuts me off with a dismissive "No." His abruptness startles me, but I am not deterred. "I was just asking because—"

"Because it would be easier for you? No. Sit," he commands, pointing at a nearby bench where pigeons gather.

"Let me explain something to you," he begins in measured, deliberate Portuguese. "I have no interest in learning English. I have no desire to go to 'BYU.' I will *never* visit your United States." He taps his chest. "I am *Brazilian*. This does not make me lesser than you. You need *me* more than I need *you*."

Mortified, I stammer out a justification: "I never meant—"

Sweat beads roll down my back. My neck and face grow hot.

"Americans—" he interjects, "set foot on Brazilian soil thinking we are primitive." He leans closer. "We are Americans, too. South Americans. When you call yourselves Americans the way you do, you erase us."

The tension is thick, and my pulse quickens.

"What should I call myself, then?" I ask hesitantly.

"You," he says as he straightens his spine, "are from Estados Unidos. Come, come, we have work to do."

I obey as a tiny smile slowly creeps across my face. He's right.

I follow him carefully through the streets that smell of roasting coffee, his reality seeping into my bones.

Brazil will teach me.

———

"Esta é minha casa," Sergio announces, gesturing proudly to a cinderblock structure with a corrugated metal roof.

Inside, the concrete floor gleams, freshly swept. His face beams with pride. A woman offers us maracujá juice (aka passionfruit). Its tropical aroma mingles with wood smoke from the cooking fire behind the house.

Elder Mouhamed and Sergio fall into rapid conversation, their words blending in a maelstrom of verbs and conjugations. My eyes dart back and forth between them as if I were watching a ping-pong match. I understand maybe one out of every 10 words.

"*Batismo,*" I hear. Baptism.

"Domingo," Elder Mouhamed confirms. Sunday.

Sergio nods enthusiastically, then Elder Mouhamed asks something I don't catch. Sergio points at him in response. Another question from Elder Mouhamed. This time, Sergio points directly at me.

My muscles tense. Elder Mouhamed's face registers surprise before settling into something more neutral.

"O que?" I ask. What?

"He wants you to perform the confirmation," Elder Mouhamed explains slowly.

The tiny cup in my hand nearly flips over from my trembling hands. "Não posso," I protest. I can't.

Sergio's smile morphs into a straight line.

"You can," Elder Mouhamed says. "And you will."

For the next three nights, I rehearse my speaking parts for the ordinance by the dim light of my dying flashlight, whispering Portuguese into the humid air. "Pelo poder do Sacerdócio de Melquisedeque." My mouth wraps around these words without issue. It's the next portion that terrifies me.

Sunday arrives before I know it. I approach the chapel with timid steps, trying hard to savor the baptismal font before me, exquisite in its simplicity. The Mormon church design is largely universal. These spaces are, above all, meeting houses with offices, classrooms for Primary to teach children under 12 and a place for Sunday worship. I love that I can enter this sacred space and encounter such familiarity.

I witness a submerged Sergio break through the water with Elder Mouhamed's hand still gripping his arm.

Following the baptism, Sergio sits at the front of the chapel, his hair still damp. I place my hands on his head, along with Elder Mouhamed and two local church members. The words I have already committed to memory flow from me easily. "Sergio Oliveira, nós o confirmamos um membro de A Igreja de Jesus Cristo dos Santos dos Últimos Dias..."

Then my mind draws a blank. I breathe in deeply, reminding myself that God is present with us at this very moment.

"E receba o Espírito Santo," I continue, "Damos-lhe uma bênção de paz."

Words I don't recognize fill the air—and they are coming from me. I perform the blessing as if I've done this before. My confidence grows with every thought that translates into Portuguese words. "Em nome de Jesus Cristo, amém," I conclude, finally opening my eyes. The room has shifted somehow.

I look up shyly, meeting Elder Mouhamed's twinkling eyes. A genuine smile spreads across his face for the first time since we met. I detect something new—recognition, even respect.

———

"You surprised me," says Elder Mouhamed on what is to be his last night in town. He folds his shirts into neat, precise stacks. Two months here, and he is already being transferred.

I look up from my journal with simple curiosity. "What did you expect?"

"I thought you might be another arrogant American," he shrugs, "like the others before you."

"Estados Unidos," I correct him with an impish smile. "I'm from the United States." He laughs at that, and it seems genuine and lighthearted. "Ah. You learn."

The next morning, I reach to shake his hand goodbye. Instead, he pulls me into a tight embrace. "You will make a great missionary," he whispers. "I am proud of you."

Elder Mouhamed might be the first person in my life who is proud of me.

I am worthy of being here.

———

Because we were too isolated to have neighbors—other than the hostile wildlife prowling the nearby mountains—I learned about pop culture through a form of osmosis with other humans. Kids at church raved about *Star Wars*—this was the early 1980s. The original *Star Wars* movies came out in the late '70s and early '80s, but pretending everything was a lightsaber showed no signs of stopping by the time the phenomenon reached me. It is clear that my parents purposefully shielded me from that fiction as much as possible.

Dad's voice boomed through our cramped living room, his hands gesticulating wildly. "*Star Wars* is Satan's design. A carefully crafted lie to make people believe good and evil spring from the same well."

"Scripture teaches us that God and Satan are *distinct*," Dad continued, his eyes blazing with the kind of certainty that disturbed me. "Light and darkness. Not two sides of the same mystical 'Force.' That's blasphemy wrapped up in special effects."

I pressed my nose against a cool windowpane at church and watched two kids battle invisible enemies—fictional to them, but very real to me.

During that Sunday's service, Brother Morrison sat in the third pew with his teenage son fidgeting beside him. I couldn't help but notice something tucked under his son's arm—something with a sleek starship on the cover.

Dad's jaw tightened. After the closing prayer, he approached Brother Morrison as if on a mission. "Brother Morrison," Dad began, his voice smooth but sharp underneath, "I couldn't help but notice your boy's reading material."

"Oh, that. It's just science fiction, nothing harmful—" Brother Morrison said, blushing.

"Nothing harmful?" Dad's eyebrows shot up. "The 'Force' is a direct assault on God. It teaches children that good and evil are two sides of the same force, rather than the eternal struggle between Heavenly Father and Lucifer."

I watched Brother Morrison's face start to register shame, then quickly polite dismissal.

My chest swelled with pride. My father was so brave for sharing the Truth. He knew that most people didn't listen when confronted with uncomfortable truths. But he was speaking on behalf of God himself.

I felt sorry for the Morrisons.

———

Elder Bassett is everything I'm not: confident, educated, quick-witted and good with analogies that simplify complex ideas. We've been companions for three months by the time we visit the Silva family.

"It's like *Star Wars,*" Elder Bassett says, leaning on a familiar analogy. "The Spirit is like the Force, right? And you can choose to use it for good, like Luke Skywalker does."

I could hear the words, but their meaning hung over me like a lead balloon. Obi-Wan Kenobi, Tatooine, the Dark Side—words and names more foreign to me than any I'd ever heard. The Silvas' teenage daughter, Maria, nods eagerly while I sit there feeling like a little boy who never received the invitation to a classmate's party.

My stomach flips. My companion is one of...*them.* A heretic.

On our walk home, I summon the courage to confront him. "Elder," I begin tentatively, "you really need to keep *Star Wars* analogies out of your teaching. My father taught me the evils of *Star Wars.* Don't you know it perverts the very nature of God?"

Elder Bassett stops walking. "What?" he says with shock. "*Star Wars* isn't evil. It has religious allegories and teaches a great lesson about the forces of good and evil. It shows you have to choose your path, defend against corruption and protect yourself from the danger of power corrupting absolutely."

I am defensive and overflowing with self-righteousness. I feel my father's certainty flow through me—a familiar, yet ill-fitting comfort. "But the Force does not come from one or the other, good or evil. We know God is good, so that is wrong. Satan is evil. That type of power doesn't have the same source."

Elder Bassett's face softens. "I see where you're coming from. But didn't Satan fall from heaven?"

"Yes."

"And don't we believe God is omnipotent?"

"Yes."

With his fingers flexing in air-quotes, he continues, "And God 'allowed' Satan to have power on earth knowing one day Christ would return to wrestle that power from him?"

"Yes."

"Well, I don't know about you, but that sounds an awful lot like the Force to me."

The pit in my stomach now feels more like a detonating bomb. My mouth opens and closes, grasping at arguments in my mind that once felt so solid. "But my dad says—"

"Your dad? *Your dad* is wrong."

I stop walking. I have never heard anyone challenge my father this way. At 20 years old, I am serving a mission thousands of miles away from home, and I am still parroting my father as if I were seven years old. The street lamp flickers, snapping me out of my temporary trance.

This blasphemy tastes...delicious.

Elder Bassett explains, "Look, you get to choose how you see things. I love *Star Wars* because the movies are incredible and the lessons are there for everyone to learn. That's my perspective. You are allowed to see things your own way, you know."

I nod as if I understand. As if I agree.

Later that evening, I struggle to find sleep. It feels as if I've outgrown the bed itself, let alone my outdated opinions and beliefs. I had already decided that my parents were crazy years ago. So why am I still burdened by their beliefs as if they are mine?

I don't think Star Wars is evil, I think with startling clarity. The thought feels dangerous and liberating, like opening the safety latch while parachuting. At that moment, I promise myself to examine my own beliefs rather than claim my parents' as my own.

With my eyes closed, I know and feel the goodness of God. His love is unmistakable and ever-present to me. I feel a peace that transcends all of my worldly clamoring, regardless of how alone I assumed I was. God has been here with me through the devastating reality of my childhood, every moment of it. He has never left. He is why I'm in Brazil, to do this work that feels so much bigger than my father's small certainties.

As I allow myself to *feel* my expanding beliefs for the first time, something extraordinary happens. My skin starts to warm as if I were standing next to a bonfire, its glow spreading over me until it touches every cell in my body. All of my senses at once feel the presence of God. This is—He is—*the Force.*

Tears flow from me and I don't try to stop them. These are tears made of something real—recognition, maybe. Love, certainly.

This feeling is one of deep affection. And it belongs to me. This isn't my father's testimony sanitized and filtered through years of repetition.

This is me, loved.

————

As a missionary in Brazil, I baptized over 70 people. My journal is thick with neatly filled pages reflecting the spiritual experiences of every single person I baptized. Maria Santos, age 34. João Silva, age 19. Ana Rodrigues, age 42. I was forever mindful of the smallest details and turns of phrase that made each encounter unique. Out of all of these beautiful encounters, one soul burns brightly in my memory: a woman who did not in fact convert.

As we turned a corner on our walk one day, my companion and I stopped abruptly in our tracks. A woman threw herself toward us, clearly in distress. "You are priests, yes?" She barely choked out her words. "Please, I beg you. Come to my house. Bless my son! He is dying!"

We followed her right then, the three of us wordlessly navigating the open sewers and dirt streets. The smell of decay twisted my stomach in knots. The streets were all just dirt roads; the gravity-fed sewage and water treatment system forced waste from every house out into open ditches along the road. The putrid water flowed ceaselessly, a constant reminder of the poverty that claimed so many citizens. The squelching sound of her flip-flops sticking and then breaking free of the newly formed mud is seared into my brain. I held my breath most of the time, realizing I needed to steady myself with slow, deep breaths. After what felt like miles, we slowed to a halt in front of a tin-roofed house that was smaller than a single-car garage.

The woman led us to a tiny room where the young boy lay motionless on a thin mattress. His breathing was tentative and labored. The rise and fall of his chest moved so slowly that it seemed like every breath might be his last. Even my breathing slowed when the heavy air began to squeeze my lungs like a vice.

We gathered around him in silence. The woman's voice cracked between sobs she was trying to control. "The Health Post is so far from here. We are out of medicine, but I can't move him. We need to get more or he will die."

She looked at us with a hopeful resignation. My companion and I let the moment settle between us, exchanging only a knowing glance. Simultaneously, we both laid hands on the boy's scorching-hot forehead. I closed my eyes to listen. A familiar ache in my stomach awakened something inside of me. I've come to know the flutters in my stomach are intuition. I spoke before I was conscious of what I was saying: "You will be healed." The woman released a heavy sob, speaking her gratitude through tears.

The next day, we came upon a group of children kicking around a half-deflated soccer ball in the middle of a deserted street. The inconsolable woman from the night before materialized in front of us as if she was an angel on high. I stared at her in disbelief.

"How is your son?" I asked with careful intention.

She paused before her smile nearly blinded me. "Why don't you ask him?"

My eyes widened as I followed her finger, pointing to a boy I didn't recognize, chasing the ball. He ran with ease, legs pumping strong and certain. This was the same boy we prayed over on his deathbed. So little time had passed since he struggled to lift his head from the pillow. I felt my knees weaken.

"That's...*him*?" My words sounded far away.

Tears pooled in her eyes as she nodded, saying, "Thank you for blessing him." I cleared my throat, unsure I could speak without my own tears flowing. I managed to invite her to come to church with us. She demurred, saying, "I have my own faith. But when I prayed to God for help, He sent you. He brought you to me in my hour of need."

We turned our gazes back to the boy kicking the soccer ball with healthy, strong legs. It was then I remembered sitting in my primary class singing songs about how God loved all His children while Wilma smiled and nodded.

When I'd come home from church, I'd overhear my parents talking about other families at church and how they didn't understand the truth. They would always smile and nod at others in public, then unleash themselves at home about the things people said and did that were wrong. Now here was this woman in front of me, a stranger of a different faith, who saw us as God's answer to her prayers. Truly, God loves all of His children unconditionally.

The seal of fear and doubt that bound me to my parents ruptured instantly.

God had helped me break free.

———

Two years later, Portuguese words became easier for me than English thoughts. I dreamed in Portuguese, prayed in Portuguese and even counted money in Portuguese. The smell of açaí and the sound of samba felt more like home than the Uintah

Basin. Whenever I closed my eyes, I heard children calling "Élder! Élder!" from their doorways.

On Preparation Day (or P-Day as we called it), fellow missionaries chattered nervously around me in my tiny apartment. They daydreamed aloud about their school schedules and rooming assignments at BYU. Their voices rose above me as I stared at my empty hands.

"What's next for you?" Elder Lloyd asked. "Are you going to BYU, too?"

The dreaded question about school haunted me for 18 years. My answer had always been, "My plan is to go on a mission." Now that my mission was ending, I had no answers.

Once the time for my departure from Brazil had arrived, I decided to seek the counsel of President Damiani, the wise church leader who was our mission president and in charge of the missionaries in our area.

"Excuse me, President Damiani," I said, my voice shaking, "I'd like to request an extension."

He considered my plea for a minute before he nodded. "One month, that's all I can approve."

President Damiani and his wife drove me to the Curitiba airport when my extension was over. They dropped me off at the same terminal where I had arrived in Brazil. I was not the same person who set foot here two years earlier. Brazil now wrapped its culture, language and spirit around me like a warm blanket.

When I touched down at the Salt Lake City airport, the December air confronted me with its harsh insistence to freeze even the snot dripping from my chilled nostrils. The announcements blared in English, my native language that was now disruptive to the Portuguese that narrated everything in my mind. When I hugged Ben and Uvene, who joined my parents to collect me at the airport, I felt a sense of comfort and ease.

Our drive home to LaPoint baffled me with its foreign roadside additions. Confused, I stared out the window at billboards advertising some kind of strange cipher I couldn't make sense of.

I heard the talk radio station crackle: "Or visit our website at H-T-T-P colon slash W-W-W dot com…"

I looked at Dad with a mixture of genuine confusion and pure curiosity. "What does that mean?"

"Well, you've got some catching up to do. The whole world moved online while you were gone." He chuckled.

"Online?"

"Geez," I thought. "Even he is talking in code." Whatever that means.

Now, this was home.

But neither of us would ever be the same.

7. ON A WING AND A PRAYER

THROUGHOUT THE MISSION, MY COMPANION AND FELLOW ELDERS and Sisters often collected college brochures, partly to dream but mostly to plan. Glossy pamphlets beckoning young people to stately brick buildings and lush campus quads were often spread across our kitchen table. I perused those pamphlets, circling application deadlines and degree programs. By the final leg of my mission, my dreams started to dissolve before my eyes. My most familiar companion—fear—clouded my internal dialogue about what I could possibly do to pursue an education.

In short order, it became clear that the first thing I had to do was get my GED.

Homeschooled students are not typically disadvantaged like my siblings and I were. My parents' errors in educating us notwithstanding, I was as curious and hungry to learn as I had ever been. If anything, I was more determined to download as much information about the world as I could. Regardless of the quality of education we did or didn't receive as homeschoolers, we were required to take the GED if we wanted to get the proper credit using the high school equivalency test.

I purchased a study guide in Vernal. When I left the bookstore, I clutched that guide so tightly against my chest, hoping its weight would somehow make things more real for me. Night after night, I read and re-read the material, highlighting and annotating obsessively. I could not fathom how to fit all of this knowledge into my head while also coordinating a proper time and place to take the test. After several days of pacing and mental preparation, I finally gathered enough courage to call the local high school.

My palm left sweat marks on the phone's receiver, evidence of my nervousness and inability to form words to get my point across. Would I find the right place to take the test? How many people would be taking it with me? I stared at the phone. After a weighted pause, my fingers started to dial Uintah High School.

"Hi, uh...I need to, uh...how do I take the GED exam?" I tripped over my anxiety as if I were 14 again and calling my girl-friend for our allotted five-minute conversation. The receptionist on the other end of the line was gracious, offering me all of the information I needed. When I hung up the phone, I was proud of myself for making it that far. I circled the test date on my calendar so many times I nearly ripped the paper underneath my red ballpoint pen.

For the next few weeks, I doubled and tripled my efforts to study the right way. I did not hesitate to burn the midnight oil, even if others in our home mocked my new pursuit.

One evening, I sat hunched over the kitchen table studying. I saw my father's shadow cast itself across the textbook in front of me. He cleared his throat: "Why do you need a GED? Is that so you can have someone tell you that you're smart?" My eyes remained on my open book. "I just want to learn." For my father, even a self-improvement on my part was a tacit indictment of him and his parenting. This was not about him or his shortcom-ings, no matter what he said.

Finally, test day arrived. I watched with fascination as my pencil moved rapidly back and forth across my answer sheet. I'm not sure what I was expecting, but it wasn't for things to go this smoothly. I'd expected some sort of indecipherable puzzle, but instead, I was greeted with questions and answers as if they were conversations I'd already had. The proctor looked up from her scoring sheet and nodded. In doing so, she acknowledged that I, Calvin Bagley, had completed my exam and was ready for it—my future—to begin. All that was left to do was march my answer sheet to her desk to release myself to fate. 21 years old, and I finally had what everyone else had at 18.

That evening, I set my certificate on the kitchen counter, propped up where a normal family would find a salt and pepper shaker, in such a way that everyone could see it. (Seasoning with pepper specifically, my parents believed, was against the Word of Wisdom—we didn't have salt and pepper shakers.)

"Passed my GED today," I crowed.

My parents remained unmoved. Dad grunted. Mom glanced at the certificate, then back to washing the dishes. "I guess your homeschooling wasn't so bad after all," she said.

My hands clenched involuntarily by my sides. I didn't want to take the bait, but the temptation was overwhelming. In an instant, memories flooded my mind: me, diving behind a bush when we heard the school bus rumble past our home, hearing neighborhood kids laughing and chatting as they walked to and from the bus stop; my body, reacquainted with the sinking feeling in my stomach whenever someone asked what grade I was in.

"Or maybe I'm just really smart and studied hard," I snapped back. I snatched the certificate off the counter and headed to my room.

I should have known better.

———

I learned piano from Cynthia and September's piano teacher when I tagged along when I was as a four- and five-year-old during their lessons. When I became the oldest at home as a 14-year-old, our mother agreed to pay for formal lessons. My piano skills progressed rapidly, so much so that I advanced to compete for a Juilliard scholarship in Utah.

The position was incredibly competitive, but I was just happy to be there. I took my qualifying performance so seriously that I threw up in the bathroom before playing. The judges gave me "special recognition," though I didn't do well enough to place. After that experience, I began to play piano at church. I taught myself how to play the organ, which has its own skill set to master. Eventually, I would lead a multi-congregational stake choir. There is a never-ending joy I find sitting down to play the piano just for the sake of making music.

When I was 15, I'd spent weeks practicing a piano piece to prepare myself to perform it at church. The piece required dexterity and quick thinking, all flying fingers and impossible reaches.

That Sunday morning, the congregation was effusive in its praise, most of them telling me how impressed they were. I played the piece in a near-perfect performance.

Afterward, Sister Huber squeezed my shoulder saying, "Great job!" I positively glowed, filled with electricity, saving my biggest-watt smile for my mother.

I took my time shaking hands and hugging well-wishers in the congregation, who echoed words of pride and admiration. When I approached my mother, I couldn't help but beam at her.

"How did I do?" I asked, sheepishly.

She smiled half-heartedly, straightening my collar. "I wish you would smile more when you play."

———

I learned through trial and error that the only way I could keep myself motivated to achieve my goals was to disconnect any expectations from my parents. They were unreliable as sources of pride in anything I would accomplish. Confidence needed to come from inside.

The day after I earned my GED, I found myself back at the bookstore. I fingered the study guides longingly, stopping on an ACT guide that was thicker than a phone book. The test, just like its accompanying manual, was twice as intimidating as the GED had been.

By this point, I had two months to prepare for the test. I had a decent handle on language arts, but math was another story. The arithmetic section was foreign and pronounced—this was a language with unfamiliar roots and perhaps not within my reach. I stared at the long division practice problem as if the numbers were ants marching across the page.

The evenings I spent studying for the ACT were fraught with stressful practice sessions as I tried daily to grasp concepts in calculus, geometry and trigonometry that were completely foreign to me. I feared that in signing up for this behemoth of a test, I had implemented the wrong calculus.

I studied as if my life depended on it because, in some ways, it did. My evenings began to blend in a blur of frantic studying, late nights reading and dinners alone with open study guides, eyes burning in the dim light.

Most of my friends were abroad in Brazil or settled into dorm rooms in Provo. If I ran into someone local at the grocery store, it was almost as if I had forgotten how to make casual conversation. Every iota of mental strength I had was devoted to my studies. Those conversations died quickly because I'd forgotten how to talk about anything other than scripture or long division. I couldn't focus on anything but catching up to my peers.

Education was our common denominator, and I wasn't adding up.

———

Of all the things that could have undermined my confidence taking the ACT—shaky times tables, questionable understanding of science, illiteracy for most of my childhood—not having the correct calculator is what nearly sent me over the edge.

I thought I had considered everything. I eyed the kid next to me intensely as he pulled out what can only be described as a remote control for space launches. It appeared he understood the assignment: purchase an outrageously expensive graphing calculator if you want to answer questions about sine, cosine and logarithmic functions.

I gripped my pencil, squeezing hard enough to give myself splinters. Teenagers surrounding me seemed lighthearted and relaxed, chatting about their plans for the weekend and their prom dates. I closed my eyes for a few moments, preparing myself for the cringiness of pulling out my dad's 10-key calculator. Cool was something I could only aspire to be, but I at least wanted to pass as normal. Slinging decades-old technology as the only adult in a room full of teenagers would almost certainly guarantee my unusualness would remain.

After four hours of mental gymnastics, I stumbled out of the classroom with a tension headache and what felt like the beginnings of carpal tunnel syndrome. I felt both defeated and exhilarated at the same time. I couldn't decide if what I was experiencing was the result of a confidence boost or self-delusion fooling me into thinking I could do anything. When the scores arrived, I got my answer. The number 16 jumped from the page aggressively, making my eyes blur. Once I was able to pull my eyes away, I folded the paper in half, then in half again and shoved it into my practice guide as a placeholder for nothing in particular.

No college would accept me with that ACT score and no high school transcripts.

I paused my disappointment long enough to help Jeff move my hastily packed boxes into a room in his new home. Jeff and his new wife, Julie, now lived permanently in Las Vegas, a city I'd come to adore. I knew on my first trip to visit Jeff in Vegas that this is where I needed to be, sooner rather than later.

My mother had begged me not to move away—and especially not to move to Las Vegas. She saw it as a city of sin, corruption and guaranteed spiritual ruin. Her fear for my soul was real and raw—especially when she saw me walk out of the door in a pair of long, baggy tan corduroy shorts (very 1996). It was the first time she had ever seen me in shorts, and her face held a perfect blend of moral panic and crushing disappointment.

I'm sure she cried as I drove away from LaPoint and into my new life.

The day I arrived, the sun was oppressively hot. The asphalt shimmered like a mirage in the middle of a July heat wave. After we hauled the last box from the car and wiped our sweaty faces, Jeff slid a Sourdough Jack sandwich from Jack in the Box across the table toward me. "Trust me. You have to try it." I was ravenous, but I'm not sure that's what made this taste so perfect; the sense of freedom, self-agency and pure bliss I now felt were even more delicious than melted cheese with tangy sauce.

I promised myself that securing a job was my number one priority. So the next morning, I drove across town targeting strip mall stores with "now hiring" signs posted in their windows. Getting in and out of the car was a challenge considering my nervousness and the outrageous heat; my skin stuck to the vinyl seats and my sweaty palms gripped the steering wheel a little too tightly. At each store, I conveyed confidence and competence.

My pitch was simple: "I'm looking for work. Do you have any openings?" The manager at Stein Mart had heard enough. "Can you start Monday?" he asked.

With my first paycheck, I bought a pair of rollerblades and decided to teach myself how to ride them. It was rough at first. I'd never had wheels under my feet—growing up in the country meant no sidewalks, no skate culture and definitely no smooth pavement. I must have looked ridiculous: a 20-something man covered in every kind of padding imaginable, from elbows to knees, wobbling down the street like a fledgling baby giraffe. But I kept at it, and eventually, I got the hang of it. I was actually pretty good and finally felt confident enough to ditch all the extra padding.

Understanding my college and social goals, Julie made it her personal mission to teach me everything she could. At the educational store Learning is Fun, she pulled a workbook from the shelf, flipping through its pages to show me what we could practice together. She pointed to multiplication tables, asking, "Do you know how to do this?"

I shook my head no, embarrassed that I hadn't been able to teach myself thoroughly enough to succeed at the ACT. She then went through workbooks for major mathematical skills, one by one, asking me directly if I knew how to do them. My answer was always "no."

By the time she picked up a workbook designed for second grade math, we found the level where I could comfortably and honestly begin. "Well, then that's where we will start," she decided.

Julie meant it when she said she would teach me everything, no matter how long her shifts at work might be. Her scrubs still smelled of hospital disinfectant when she sat down with me one night to explain several options I had to move forward with a plan for college. She drew simple diagrams on napkins, creating a kind of flow chart that featured boxes for semesters, arrows for prerequisites and numbers for the amount of credits I would need at each level.

When my first University of Nevada Las Vegas rejection letter arrived, she knew to open it before I could. "Okay. Then our work is not done," she said. She called the admission office to set up an appointment for me, no ifs, ands or buts.

I worked hard to fight back my inherent feelings of shame— of being undereducated, of waiting as long as I did to try to matriculate—in order to focus on what the counselor had to say.

Her office was neat and minimally decorated, several framed

diplomas covering the walls. She studied me carefully as I answered her questions about my educational background. I leaned toward her, breathlessly recounting my brush with home-schooling, studying for my GED and working full time since I was a child.

After a few minutes, she pulled out a thick folder and plopped it on the desk in front of her. She scooted forward in her chair, tapping her pen against her lips as if in deep thought. "Two semesters as a non-admitted student with a 2.0 GPA, mini-mum, and I can admit you." She slid papers across the desk for me to sign.

"I can do that," I promised her.

As a child, time moved at a glacial pace. Then it was suddenly as if I'd blinked my eyes and seconds later, 22 flickering candles adorned a chocolate cake the Edingtons bought me for my birthday.

Wayne Edington, Julie's father, sang Happy Birthday in a deep baritone. Six of the Edington kids crowded around him at the kitchen table, each of their voices distinct. Julie said, "Make a wish." Instinctively, I closed my eyes to picture my wish.

For a few moments, I realized all of the wishes I'd had so far in my life were all coming true at that moment. I now knew what it felt like to belong and to be part of a family.

One of the key milestones I missed as a child was learning how to swim. My father once suggested that the quickest way to learn was to throw me into the deep end of a lake—but I failed that test at scout camp. I'd seen him sloppily doggy paddle through the water, his lack of grace being just one of many signs that maybe I ought to find a better swimmer to teach me such an important skill.

The diving board bounced under my awkward feet. I hopped once, twice, then several more times as I bided my time, amping myself up enough to jump into the turquoise water.

I gazed admiringly at Julie treading water below, studying how she plunged under the water, popping right back up to smooth her wet hair back into a slick ponytail. "Just remember what I showed you about holding your nose," she instructed me. I began my cannonball countdown by muttering cues under my breath: "Jump in three…two…one—" I surprised myself by leaping before I'd finished counting. Water rushed in over my head, muffling my squeal of glee. The tip of my toes touched the bottom of the pool, then I coiled myself into a squat before I sprang back up to the top.

I broke the surface with one loud gasp, spitting out the mouthful of water I'd gulped on my swim up to dry land. I felt like a bubble popping up in an effervescent soda can. I felt Julie's hands grip my arms, steadily guiding me toward the edge of the pool.

"Again," she said, "keep trying. It gets easier."

I swallowed my fair share of chlorine in those summer months. Day after day, I'd push myself off from the pool wall, practicing my free stroke without stopping. I waded in the shallow end for several minutes between doing my laps to help build up my stamina. I knew the contained perimeter of the pool was no match for the unpredictable nature of an ocean, but my strength as a swimmer progressed nonetheless. I just needed to have the chance to learn. I became more teachable the more I learned, whether it was the breaststroke or algebra.

———

My eyes flew open with a start, my brain momentarily confused at how late I had slept in. Christmas morning was finally here, greeting me with the scent of cinnamon rolls baking and the sound of wrapping paper being ripped in two.

I made my way into the Edingtons' living room, careful not to interrupt traditions that were not mine to observe. The first thing I saw when the living room came into view was a stocking with my name on it. My throat tightened with a sudden wave of unfamiliar emotions. Jeff handed me a box, telling me to grab the heavy rectangle with both hands. Inside, I unfolded a jacket made of shiny leather that gleamed like slick oil. I lifted the jacket to inspect this unusual item, running my hands over its smooth surfaces.

"This is..." my voice cracked and my eyes shifted to the floor. As a 22-year-old, I was only now experiencing my very first real Christmas morning. I buried my face in Jeff and Julie's shoulders, unable to quell my tears or find the right words to say.

That fall, I attended UNLV as a non-admitted student, having never experienced a single day of school in my life. I signed up for Spanish, English, math and business courses. I handily bombed the math placement exam, ensuring I would spend the next two semesters in remedial classes. But I did not let that small detail keep me from eventually achieving a 4.0 GPA after my first two semesters. I was so proud of myself, I taped my grades to the refrigerator as if I were one of Jeff and Julie's kids posting a drawing.

The LDS Institute of Religion at UNLV boasted its own unique hum, the sound of pool cues clinking and students laughing in the hallways on their way to religion classes. On an otherwise uneventful weekday, that is where I first saw her: Karissa, a luminous sight in the middle of a gaggle of other college freshmen. Her warmth radiated from across the room. I hadn't yet met her formally, but I felt I needed to know her. She intimidated me, though not in a negative way. We were both in our first semester of college, but I was 22 and she was 17. She seemed to have tons of friends of varying ages, and she was always at the center of a group of people. I had developed a few friends within the Institute choir, but I didn't yet know how to manage a full social life.

By the spring, I started to feel claustrophobic. The lecture halls began to feel too crowded, and my ability to concentrate waned. I became restless and unsure of myself, feelings I still had not shaken. One day, a friend asked me to come with him as he packed his car for a move to Logan, Utah. "Where else do you have to be?" he asked. "Logan is beautiful. It'll be a fresh start."

I weighed all of the progress I had made—my 4.0, real friends, Sunday dinners with the Edingtons—all of that was here in Nevada. I loved to learn, but the strictures of formal schooling were a difficult thing for me to adapt to. I decided to go, not realizing I was running away from security. How long and how far would I run?

———

I secured a full-time job within days of arriving in Logan working the swing shift at the Icon Health and Fitness treadmill factory. I exhibited exactly zero characteristics that might make me a good fit for the job. Nevertheless, I carried on with the confidence of a much bigger and speedier young man. My first task was to pull extremely heavy treadmills off of the assembly line and push them into individual stalls to be tested.

Either by design or by coincidence, the manager hired incredibly cute girls to test those same treadmills. Different groups of attractive young women filtered in and out, running on the new treadmills every week. Their ponytails swishing back and forth mesmerized me for long stretches at a time. I couldn't help but stare, mouth agape, at this vision before me. I had never been more painfully aware of my lanky frame or the now-apologetic mass of all 140 pounds of me. Years of poor nutrition had shaped my body—thin, underdeveloped, and starved of protein during the most critical times of growth. My body simply hadn't had the fuel it needed to build itself properly.

A few weeks into the job, it became clear that I was not exactly up to the task of moving such heavy equipment for any real distance.

One night, I lost control of an exceptionally large treadmill as I tried to move it, watching helplessly as it toppled to its side, crashing onto the ground straight off of the assembly line. The near-constant vibrations of the factory floor ground to a halt under my feet. The assembly line stopped, then all of the workers looked up at me with disgust and frustration. I couldn't blame them—their bonuses depended entirely on piece production, which I had all but guaranteed they would not earn that day.

The next day, my boss took me off the line and plunked me in a stall. Already punching above my weight class, I cringed at the thought of exerting more effort and burning more calories than I already was. The last thing my skinny body needed was more exercise. I still played basketball regularly, but as a treadmill tester, I was simply a non-starter. I was embarrassed, but quickly sucked it up. Thankfully, another employee alerted me to a job opening in the Plastics division of the factory—on the graveyard shift, no less. There wouldn't be beautiful young women there to keep me company, but the middle-aged workers next to me did just fine.

My Utah State University acceptance letter appeared on the kitchen table as if by magic—a transfer offer from UNLV that I was genuinely proud of. I had done it. I was a bona fide college student. I eagerly flipped through the course catalog, only to find that nearly every class I wanted or needed was already marked "closed." It was too late in the year to get what I needed. Frustrated, I crumpled the letter and stuffed it into a drawer.

By the next semester, I was tossing my belongings into garbage bags, ready to make another exit at a moment's notice.

"Of course you can stay with us," Belinda said excitedly. "Don is already clearing out the basement."

———

Belinda lived with her husband, Don, an hour's drive south down I-15 in Bountiful, Utah. I was excited to live with them, but not before I tried my hand at one tradition I wanted to partake in before I left.

I made a beeline for the campus, the full moon illuminating the dark sky above and the ground below like a spotlight. The famed Block A statue stood at the center of hundreds of students sprawled across the Utah State campus quad. Nearly everyone was paired up, the crowd mostly couples whispering to each other as they lazed on their blankets. I was part of the pack of wolves circling the statue hunting for their "True Aggie" moment. I loitered uncomfortably with my hands shoved in both pockets, carefully watching exactly what everyone else around me was doing.

I scanned the crowd for a few minutes. A girl with auburn hair pulled into a messy bun caught my eye almost by accident. She was only about 20 feet away, but I felt as though we were already inches apart. I noticed her shifting nervously from foot to foot, which I found endearing.

She looked as nervous as I felt. I started walking toward her, and then she bit her lower lip and decided she might join me. We climbed the steps of the Block A statue together, both of us aware that the moonlight was overwhelmingly romantic in the way it cast our shadows on the lawn just ahead of us. In an instant, our eyes met and we wasted no time, leaning in for a kiss. She immediately put her hand to her mouth, giggling to herself.

"What's your name?" she asked.

I chuckled, then coyly replied, "Wouldn't it be better if you never knew?" She seemed surprised, then nodded her head.

With the faint taste of cherry lip gloss on my lips, I turned and walked away.

————

The first thing Belinda asked me when I set my bags down was "Are you hungry? I made turkey sandwiches."

She fussed over me in a way that made me feel enormous comfort. I happily accepted the glass of milk and plate of food she presented me, eternally grateful that someone other than myself cared this much about how I was doing. She never seemed to stop moving, always bustling around the house with urgency. Within five minutes of me being in her home, she smoothed my hair, adjusted my collar and reminded me that I was her little brother—someone worth fussing over.

Now that I had a new place to lie my head down at night, I moved forward with finding a new job. I worked at a chemical supply store, which reeked of bleach and something else, I'm assuming, much more toxic. Customers rarely made eye contact with me behind the counter when they checked out. I never asked why they needed such specific industrial-strength supplies, and they never offered an explanation.

When a man with a drug-addled disposition and a mouth full of rotted teeth asked for his third bulk order of hydrochloric acid in a week, I started to connect the dots. The mysterious containers that lined our shelves seemed to hide darker purposes than what met the untrained eye.

My supervisor observed this transaction with a smirk that never left his face. He slapped me on my back and said, "Great business, right? The cops love us because we help them track these idiots."

I tried to force a smile, but the writing was on the periodic table—it was time to look for another job.

When I got home after work, I found Don sprawled on the couch, still wearing his Delta flight attendant uniform. He seemed especially relaxed as he loosened his tie and tossed his name badge on the coffee table. He must have noticed me eyeing him curiously because he started to regale me with stories about his time in the sky. "You should try it. You could travel and meet a ton of new people. All you'll have to do is get really good at balancing while not spilling scalding hot coffee on yourself or anyone else," he laughed.

I agreed he might have a point, so I applied to become a flight attendant with Delta, United and American Airlines.

Sometime later, I practically jumped out of my skin at the sound of the landline's shrill ring. An airy, pleasant voice greeted me when I picked up the receiver: "Is this the applicant who speaks fluent Portuguese?"

My breath caught in my throat and my heart threatened to hammer itself out of my chest. "Yes, this is him."

"I am calling from United Airlines because we'd like you to come to Denver to test for the position."

I nodded reflexively, almost forgetting to accept her invitation. "Great. I'll be there."

After Denver, United Airlines flew me to their headquarters in Chicago located in an unassuming building next to the O'Hare airport. Despite my nerves, I nailed my interview, after which the facilitator offered me the position on the spot. I felt the electricity course through my system, and I didn't try to play it cool. My smile stretched so wide across my face that it hurt to hold it in place—but I managed to do that just fine.

Belinda met me at the Salt Lake City airport doors where I greeted her with a hug and my announcement: "I got the job!"

She dropped her purse from her shoulder to wrap me up in a hug so tight she nearly lifted me off the ground. "I knew you could do it. I am so proud of you," she squealed.

The plan was to attend training for two months with United —unpaid. I knew without those paychecks to count on I wouldn't be able to afford my car any longer. I calculated that risk and decided it was well worth it.

A month later, UAL flew me back to Chicago to begin flight attendant training. I called it training, but all my new friends called it Barbie Bootcamp.

A shuttle bus picked me up from O'Hare airport to take me to the training facility. I watched dozens of other trainees arrive, gathering around their luggage protectively. Accents from every corner of the U.S. mixed into one mellifluous sound of nervous excitement. I stood by myself, happy to observe all of the happy conversations happening among new coworkers.

A Black and Cuban woman with large almond eyes smiled so warmly at me that I thought for a moment she recognized me as someone she knew. "Hi, I'm Tammy," she said confidently, offering her hand, "it's so nice to meet you." I detected a hint of what I learned was her Miami accent in the cadence of her speech, each word a staccato note imbued with vibrancy and color.

Within a few minutes of small talk, she had already introduced me to other trainees who formed a circle around us. Hector from Puerto Rico caught my attention. He spoke sharp English, his thick accent adding a kind of flourish to every sentence. The group closed itself in a circle organically, due in no small part to Tammy's magnetic energy. I couldn't stop myself from smiling.

And with that introduction, my head stayed firmly fixed in the clouds.

———

My glossy badge hung proudly from its lanyard, gently tapping against my chest as I walked with purpose down the dormitory hallway. Thirty strangers, suitcases in hand, excitedly clustered around doorways. A blue badge gleaming from each person's chest—blue was our class color, identifying us for the next six and a half weeks. In the cafeteria, more seasoned trainees wore colors like green and red. Our blue cohort clustered together, exchanging knowledge about rules and gossiping about who might get cut.

I outgrew my shyness somewhere between the Curitiba airport and my treadmill debacle. So when it came time for me to make new friends, I was motivated to do so.

I pushed open the propped door of my dorm room, room 247, where three men stood around unpacking their suitcases, ready to socialize. They greeted me warmly, each shaking my hand. Wesley was the first person I met. It seemed as if he had stepped off of the cover of a Brooks Brothers catalog with his coif sculpted artfully, not a single hair out of place.

Next, I noticed JB's elaborate set of rings glinting in the fluorescent light. He grabbed my hand and exclaimed, "Virgin Islands, baby!" His smile was infectious.

Damon spoke with a friendly Dallas drawl that softened every word. He was born in Ireland, so his accent drew out the brogue when he was especially animated. He looked like David Spade when he fixed his hair, tucking strands behind his ear. "This is gonna be awesome, y'all."

Before I knew it, three weeks passed by in a whirlwind. One morning, JB's desk chair sat empty during our daily briefing. I glanced around expecting to see him slide in late trying to go unnoticed, but when he hadn't returned by the afternoon, I knew something had happened. When I got back to our room later, his bed was stripped bare and none of his flashy rings cluttered the top of his dresser. None of his flamboyant, patterned shirts hung in the closet, either. I noticed Wesley sitting on his bed, staring despondently into empty space. "Broke conduct rules," he said quietly. "That's all they'll tell us."

I was forced to learn too early in my life not to get overly attached to anyone; I knew what it meant to be at a permanent loss. But this stung, nonetheless.

I would miss my friend.

———

The 767 engines growled beneath my feet as the ambient light of Frankfurt's unassuming city line slowly disappeared from view. I was on my international training flight. I spent 36 hours in Europe in this, my first trip across the Atlantic. It was then that I discovered how to enjoy my own company. I wandered the city's cobblestone streets alone, brushing my hands along medieval walls, biting into a bratwurst I purchased from street vendors and pinching myself along the way. I could not believe this was my job—that this was my life.

But my sadness returned when Damon's empty bed greeted me in my Chicago dorm room. I spotted Hector in the common room, crying in Tammy's arms.

"Damon overslept," Tammy whispered. "That's all it was. And he missed his Paris flight."

Damon, a person who knew every aircraft model by its engine sound, had dreamed of flying since he was a child. And he slept through his dream.

———

Don's hands trembled slightly as he pinned the silver wings to my uniform jacket. "I'm so proud of you," he said. His flight attendant's smile flashed momentarily, but I knew it was genuine. I traced the wings on my chest with complete elation. It was official now. I was a real flight attendant.

I rented a studio apartment near O'Hare that felt so much like the dorm room at United. It had an antiseptic, sterile, temporary and lonely vibe within every one of its square inches. Late-night or early-morning phone calls became a regular occurrence. My pager would buzz at 4 am, then I'd call ops to get my orders: "Report to O'Hare in two hours for a five-day assignment." I'd grab my already-packed bag to disappear into the sky.

The intrigue never dampened with each new city or country, but my returning days became more difficult. I'd turn the key in the door lock, stepping into my apartment with relief, only to find a coating of dust collected on the coffee table and expired milk in the fridge. I wasn't sure this was how I wanted to live. When I called Tammy, her laugh warmed me through the phone.

"Come crash with us. Don't stay there by yourself."

Tammy's apartment was bigger, louder and much more fun than mine. Even before stepping into her two-bedroom apartment, the hallway pulsed with life. She lived there with five other flight attendants, though their schedules rotated them in and out so frequently it was almost as if she lived there by herself. Suitcases lined the hallway like preschoolers waiting their turn to board a bus. The refrigerator was host to a cornucopia of ethnic foods, all leftovers from exotic travels.

Hector was as vibrant as Tammy. He taught me salsa steps in the living room while Tammy critiqued our skills from the kitchen. We were young and foolish and in love with spending as much time together as we could. I'd often get quiet when the music was loud, sometimes just to meditate on my good fortune with gratitude. These were my friends.

———

Strapped into my jump seat, our plane slowly descended toward the Orlando International Airport. Out of the corner of my eye, I saw a middle-aged woman frantically waving from row 12. Her face was pressed forcefully against the window, hands waving absurdly. There was real panic in her eyes—terror, even.

I undid the straps across my chest and lap to get to her quickly. When I knelt beside her to ask how I could help, she asked, "Are we still going to Orlando?" Her voice was jittery and deadly serious. I glanced at the window across her shoulder where I could see the plane circling for its approach.

"Yes ma'am, we are."

She pointed forcefully at the lights below, shouting, "Well, we just passed it!"

She was as serious as the heart attack she was in the process of causing herself, but I had to stifle my laughter.

I bit my lip to keep from laughing. "The plane will often circle before it lands," I told her quickly, turning as soon as I felt my face break.

By the time I made it back to my jumpseat, I fell apart in hysterics. When I heard her breathe a huge and extremely audible sigh of relief, I completely lost my composure. I still wonder to this day if she ever caught on to her mistake or realized how hilariously ridiculous it was.

Hector was a great social director for our crew. He monitored flight times and destinations like it was his Fantasy Football League. His fingers flew across his laptop keyboard in our kitchen, the place that quickly became our favorite place to hang out.

"Guys, listen: there's a 767 to Denver leaving in 40 minutes. First class is empty, there's a lunch service, then we can catch the new 777 back in time for dinner." He looked up with his trademark mischievous, Cheshire cat grin. "Who wants to dine in the sky with me today?"

Twenty minutes later, we were all three of us sprinting through O'Hare gripping standby tickets like teenagers with full bank accounts and no responsibilities.

I loved waking up in the apartment I shared with Tammy and Hector. Sometimes on Sunday mornings, I'd lie in bed listening intently as the church bells rang across the city. I hadn't bothered to set my alarm, though I felt some guilt about it. By noon, I would have agreed to meet Tammy and Hector out at whatever club was having a day party. I never grew tired of feeling the bass thump before we even reached the doors to enter.

Strobe lights flashed across a sea of young people packed together on the dance floor. No matter the time of day or day of the week, I always nursed the same drink: a Coke with ice that I somehow made last more than three hours at a time on a regular basis.

I got such a kick out of observing my friends weave their way in and out of openings in the crowd, always hand-in-hand. Tammy would lean close to my ear, shouting almost incoherently over the music: "Did you see what happened to Marcus last night?" I would nod, whether I heard who she was talking about or not. I enjoyed living vicariously through these melodramas, as long as they left me out of them.

Our group of flighty friends moved through the city like a traveling comedy troupe. Whenever our days off lined up— sometimes even four or five days in a row—we'd pile into someone's apartment without a plan or a care in the world. We were willing to see where the day or days might take us.

"Movies?" Hector would ask as he draped himself lazily over the couch cushions.

"Movies!" Tammy and I would shriek in unison, looking at each other and laughing.

I always volunteered to be the guy wearing a trench coat, carefully concealing items like a large pizza box or opened bulk candy bags I'd smuggle underneath. I didn't mind the burning heat from the fresh pizza during the Chicago winter, even if it made my ribs hurt. By the time we'd make it to our theater seats, the pizza was unrecognizable in its box.

"That does not look appetizing," Tammy whispered, stifling her laughter.

"Still tastes like pizza," Hector would reply, greedily snatching up lopsided slices two at a time.

Back at our apartment, Tammy would set up a makeshift salon in the bathroom. She'd wrap a towel around my shoulders and angle my head forward over the sink. Her scissors made a frantic snipping sound that always made me nervous that my ears might become collateral damage even though I knew she was a trained cosmetologist. She nipped at my unkempt hair with precision and efficiency every time.

Our other flight attendant friends would line up for their turn at a Tammy cut and color, turning the bathroom into a full-scale salon. There was a near-constant sound of air blasting from the blow dryer, and by the end of the night, the floor would be covered with hair of every different color.

The next time I visited Belinda, she inspected my haircut, walking in a 180-degree circle. "Who did this?" she asked, running her fingers through the new layers.

"Tammy cuts my hair now," I stammered without thinking.

Belinda's neutral face fell into a frown. For years, she had been the only cosmetologist in my life, fussing over how I looked. She took pride in helping me stay well-groomed, and she always made sure to tell me how handsome I looked. Now, it seemed, I had replaced her with someone she'd never met. She looked at me once again, gathering up her disappointment and stowing it away to be dealt with at another time.

"It looks really nice," she said, after a long stretch of silence, but her voice was small and sounded hurt, and she didn't offer to trim my hair or fix anything if I needed it.

———

The first time we experienced snow in Chicago, Tammy called me in a panic.

"How am I supposed to get my car out of the parking lot?"

she exclaimed. "The more I hit the gas, the more the wheels spin in place."

It took me a few minutes to reach her, and by the time I did, she had fallen into a full-blown panic. I found her sitting in her car, hands gripping the steering wheel, her eyes closed and the tires revving and whining against the packed snow and ice. I knocked on her window gently and gestured for her to roll it down.

"Move over," I said, "I'm going to show you something."

I had her place her hands on top of mine on the steering wheel—10 o'clock and two o'clock. "Don't fight the snow," I instructed, "work with it. If you feel the wheels start to slip and they make that sound like before, don't gun it. Just back off of the gas and try again."

After a few good practice rounds, her breathing finally slowed. "In Miami, we didn't have to deal with any of *this*," she said, gesturing wildly around her. "Our snowstorms were hurricanes." She laughed uncomfortably, then finally leaned back in her seat to relax. "But, we also didn't get to build snowmen like that," she said, pointing to kids playing across the street.

I remember how Tammy looked every time we walked by a store's Christmas display in the window. Her eyes would widen as if she were seeing someone perform a magic trick for the first time. She'd always stop in front of the windows to study the elaborate and festive decorations.

On Christmas Eve, I prepared stockings for my roommates to surprise them. It mattered to me that they felt warmth and comfort when they woke up on Christmas morning. I knew from the stories Tammy told me that her family didn't celebrate Christmas or other holidays, which always made me feel a little sad.

I was uniquely qualified to speak to that kind of disappointment as a child, so I figured maybe we could start our own traditions. I woke up early Christmas morning to see their reactions when my friends saw "Santa Claus" had come to visit.

Tammy was the first to wake up. She was surprised to find a stocking with her name on it. She looked at it for a few moments without opening anything, then walked over to hug me without saying a word.

We would make our own joy.

———

Weekends in Chicago allowed me to rebuild my identity.

After a few months, I started to feel like something was missing from my life. It didn't take long to realize it was church. I found my assigned ward in Chicago and started going again. That's where I met Keenan, on my first Sunday. He was also a flight attendant with United, just a year ahead of me, and the first person I'd ever met from Hawaii. We connected over our love of music and the fact that we were both single. He had a beautiful voice and played the ukulele, the upright bass and guitar. We sang both church hymns and contemporary songs, harmonizing our voices like we had been singing together for years.

Outside of church, I was also falling in love with the music of the time—especially the wave of late-'90s alternative rock that filled the air in Chicago. Keenan and I, along with a rotating cast of friends, went to concerts at every venue we could—Foo Fighters, Filter, Bush and Blink 182 at Twisted 6 in the United Center, and bands like Better Than Ezra, Counting Crows and Creed at the House of Blues. But no band meant more to me than Smashing Pumpkins. When I won the lottery to attend their "final" show at the United Center, I felt like I had hit the jackpot. Billy Corgan opened with a haunting acoustic and piano set, then returned with the band to absolutely tear the roof off. They played for hours. At the time, I felt like it wasn't just a concert—it was one of the best nights of my life.

Back at church, I began teaching a primary class for seven-year-olds at our ward, where I committed to teaching every other week to fit my flight schedule as it was.

One Sunday, I wore my treasured leather jacket Jeff and Julie gifted me when I lived with them. One of the kids was positively spellbound when he saw me, almost as if I were a movie star. After class, I was in the hallway when he ran up to me excitedly, dragging his mother by the hand behind him.

He said proudly while pointing at me, "Mommy, mommy! This is my teacher and he's a bad man!" He thought leather jackets were reserved only for bikers in gangs like the Hell's Angels.

I loved those kids.

Flying for work stirred something in me—something big. I decided I didn't just want to serve drinks at 30,000 feet. I wanted to be the one in the cockpit. I signed up for flight instruction at a regional airport in Schaumburg, Illinois, just outside Chicago. I trained on a Piper Warrior, a small underwing plane that seated four. Flying that tiny aircraft felt like paddling a canoe in the sky —light, exposed and wildly thrilling. I loved it.

My progress was slow. Flight school was expensive, and I was living on a meager flight attendant salary. But I kept going, eking out lessons between trips and scraping together whatever money I could. I believed this could be my future.

Years later, I'd come to understand something about myself that I didn't know then: as much as I loved flying, being a commercial pilot would've been a terrible job fit for me. Flying professionally is all about structure—routines, rules and checklists. I've never been great with repetition. I struggle driving the same route to work two days in a row.

So while I still love flying, I'm glad that dream didn't work out the way I imagined. I was chasing freedom but I would've ended up locked in a cockpit.

I quickly learned how to structure my days off as a flight attendant to make room for even more travel. I'd take off the last week of one month and the first week of the next, using the time

I'd accumulated to visit Brazil and reconnect with people from my mission, see Jeff and Julie who had moved to Southern California, or spend time with Belinda in Salt Lake City.

————

The wind whipped across Oceanside Beach as I pulled my sleeves down over my hands as Jeff, Julie and I strode across the sand. We'd only meant to go out for a walk, maybe collect a few shells. But when we reached the water's edge, I stopped. I'd never touched the ocean before.

The waves thundered against the shore with such power it felt as if a freight train were passing in front of us. The waves crashed on top of themselves, sending spray that stung my eyes. My sneakers sank into the wet sand as foam rushed toward my feet, a constant approach and retreat holding its power over me.

I was falling in love with the ocean on my first visit.

I reached down to unlace my shoes, dipping one toe to test the temperature. Before long, I had submerged both of my feet into the water. Julie raised an eyebrow. "Are you sure about that? It's freezing."

But I was already moving forward. The water bit at my ankles, shooting pain up my leg, yet I couldn't pull away. I stepped deeper into the surf, my jeans dampening at the cuffs.

"I can't believe you're actually doing this," Julie laughed, but she was already rolling up her pants. "Come on then—if you're going in, we're all going in."

Jeff shook his head, grinning, as he peeled off his jacket. "Here's to nothing!"

We waded deeper in the darkening waves. The smaller waves grew with powerful momentum the further away we moved from shore, their green walls of water crashing on and around our heads. One wave hit me square in the chest, knocking me down. Salt water flooded my mouth and burned my nostrils.

"Here comes a big one!" Julie shouted.

The wave lifted us off our feet for a moment before slamming us back down. I gasped, spit salt, and immediately started laughing. Jeffs's head popped up from the water, his hair plastered to his head as if he had slicked it back with gel.

"This is crazy!" he yelled—but he was grinning, too.

We stayed until our lips turned blue and our fingers cramped from the cold. When we finally stumbled out, our soaked clothes clung to our skin, and we left dark footprints in the sand back to the car. Jeff cranked the heat while Julie wrung water from her hair and I tried unsuccessfully to squeeze out my shirt.

And with that, I made my peace with open water and the ocean.

———

Three months later, I stood in Keenan's mother's kitchen on Oahu's North Shore, watching her hands move smoothly as she cubed fresh ahi. "Try," she said, holding out a piece of poke on her finger. The fish melted on my tongue. Through the window, I could see Waimea Beach stretching like a crescent moon, its waves smaller and less aggressive today than the giants I remembered from Oceanside.

Keenan's fiancée, Rebekeh, hadn't been able to join us—she was back in Chicago, working as a nanny.

Keenan appeared with two boogie boards under his arm, his easy smile making me feel instantly welcome in their home.

The sand at Waimea was unlike anything I'd ever imagined—softer, whiter, warm between my toes. Keenan demonstrated the stance, lying flat on the board with practiced ease.

"Watch my hands," he said, gripping the front edges. "And remember—don't fight the wave. Let it carry you."

I copied his position, the foam pressing cold against my stomach through my rash guard. A wave approached, small but still intimidating. Keenan yelled telling me when to go.

Suddenly I was flying. The board shot forward, water spraying past my face as I gripped the edges. The wave carried me toward shore, and for those few seconds, I wasn't fighting anything—I was part of something larger, riding the ocean's rhythm instead of battling against it. I could feel the strength of my trust in Keenan.

When the wave finally deposited me in the shallows, I lay there in the foam, looking up at the sky. Keenan jogged over, his board under his arm.

"Lullei, yeah?" he said, using the mellifluous Hawaiian word so effortlessly.

I nodded, saltwater still dripping from my hair.

Beautiful, yes.

Fast forward a few months and instead of the warmth of Hawaii, it was a crisp, snowy day just after Christmas. Keenan and Rebekeh were married in the Chicago temple, fresh snow piled neatly along the sidewalks, the kind that makes everything feel new. At their reception that night, they asked me to play the piano and sing Jim Brickman's "The Love I Found in You" during their first dance.

Being part of that moment—watching two friends I loved begin their life together, and knowing they had chosen me to help mark that moment—was something I carried with quiet pride. I hadn't always felt like I belonged in other people's joy. But that night, I did.

———

Cynthia's cap sat crooked atop her head when she walked across the stage in Kaiserslautern, Germany. There she strode, the first Bagley to earn a college degree. I whooped from the audience, a typical American not caring if the buttoned-up German professors in the next row looked down their noses at me.

That night in her apartment the size of a postage stamp, we watched *Saving Private Ryan* on her small TV. Despite my informal study of pop culture, I was still shockingly ignorant about history and geography. There we were, Americans in Germany, watching a fictionalized account of history play out in the exact place where it happened.

My life felt electric. I was loving every part of it—jet-setting around the world as a flight attendant, discovering new cities like I was making up for lost time. I even bought a special bag that clipped onto the back of my Travelpro Rollerboard just to carry my rollerblades. With wheels at the ready, I could explore almost any city the moment I landed. It wasn't always easy—Paris, for example, was a nightmare on cobblestone—but I still did it. I rollerbladed from my hotel to the Arc de Triomphe, down the Champs-Élysées, past the Eiffel Tower and all the way to Notre Dame. I felt completely free—like I was writing my own story on the pavement of cities I never dared to dream I'd see.

———

The flight attendant lounge clock glowed at 11:47 pm. I was halfway through a four-hour standby shift at O'Hare, wondering where I could be sent at this late hour. "The San Francisco transfer window closes at midnight," I heard on the intercom.

My fingers moved before my brain registered what I was doing, clicking through tabs on the shared terminal. I furiously typed my employee number, hit submit and held my breath. The decision I had just made without any thought gave me the feeling that I was tip-toeing precariously on the precipice of a cliff. The next morning, my phone beeped with a message from United: "Transfer approved, effective in two weeks."

Guilt gripped my heart when I saw Tammy's face crumple with disappointment.

"But we just got the perfect setup," she moaned, gesturing around at our messy and wonderful apartment. Hector shook his head in the kitchen, telling me, "Man, you're crazy."

Here I was, a grown man—debatable in my emotional life—

but an adult all the same, repeating a pattern that once baffled me. I was impervious to their pain. When I met Tammy and Hector, I knew I loved them instantly. But a tiny echo in the back of my mind reminded me that I still did not matter, and I had to keep running.

Like Pinocchio, I was not yet a real boy. Not to myself, anyway.

Though my new friends were very important to me, *they* were not real, either. It would be years before I learned "The Heart's Filthy Lesson," as David Bowie once sang it. I mattered, and so did the people I loved—

"But the heart has its own memory and I have forgotten nothing," as Albert Camus once said.

New Year's Eve hurtled toward me at 35,000 feet over the Atlantic while I served champagne to passengers.

Most of them probably thought they were exceptionally clever by noting that we were "flying into the future" for Y2K.

As we approached Charles de Gaulle at 1 a.m. Paris time, my breath caught in my throat at the beauty outside my jumpseat window. Hundreds of millions of lights sparkled like freshly polished diamonds.

Our crew stumbled forward, arms linked, drinking in the sight of the Eiffel Tower. We were jetlagged and punch-drunk from the time change, but filled with happiness. Twenty thousand lights greeted us, twinkling across its wrought-iron lattice. We had unknowingly arrived on the very night those lights sparkled for the first time. What would become one of the most iconic images in the world had just been born—and we were there to witness it.

We stood there in the cold, shivering or vibrating with excitement—*Il fait un froid de canard*—it is duck cold, as the locals say.

I smiled to myself, knowing full well that this was exactly where I was supposed to be—

Et ainsi de suite—and so on, or so it goes, the pattern repeats itself.

————

On a day like any other, the 767's engines wound down to a low rumble as we sat on the runway's edge at O'Hare. I leaned my forehead against the jump seat window, half-watching other planes taxi past us toward the gates we should have left behind. Time slowed to a cruel stop. Five minutes ticked by. Ten.

"We apologize for the delay," the captain's voice thundered over the intercom. "We're experiencing a ground stop. More updates to follow as soon as we have them."

Tammy caught my eye across the galley with a nervous look. This was the first time she and I were ever assigned a flight together and we were excited to have a layover in Los Angeles.

I shrugged—ground stops happen. There could be bad weather anywhere, even in Los Angeles, or any number of air traffic control issues. I didn't feel worried. But something troubled me in Tammy's furtive glance. The quiet on the radio would be our first sign something was amiss, the way the control tower had fallen silent.

"We've learned that a plane hit a building in New York City," the captain blurted out to the entire cabin thirty minutes later. Still, my mind did not register what was happening. I pictured a small Cessna clipping the tip of a skyscraper, or perhaps a banner plane accidentally flying off course. The passengers stirred in their seats, restless but not yet panicked.

Then came the second announcement: "Now, we've heard that another aircraft hit a second building in New York City."

The captain's voice sounded shaky this time.

Passengers reached for their phones to turn them on,

ignoring or forgetting it was forbidden while the plane was taxi-ing. I did not correct them.

One, two, then dozens of ringtones chimed with voice mails, texts, emails and RSS feed alerts on BlackBerry phones.

I watched as a woman in 14C held her phone to her ear, color instantly draining from her face. "Wait, the Twin Towers?" she whispered, her voice growing louder, "*Both* towers?! But my son works there. David works there." She hung up, then immediately began dialing. One attempt after another was met with the busy signal's mocking beeps.

A man wearing a traditional keffiyeh beckoned angrily at Tammy, his broken English harsh from his frustration. "Connection in Los Angeles. Miss connection!" He didn't understand why the crew sat there motionless, why his travel was so abruptly halted. Other passengers looked up from their phones watching him closely, their eyes hardening with suspicion at every other Arabic word.

A woman in 18F stood up, pointing and yelling, "Tie him up! You need to restrain him right now."

Her mania pitched higher with every ignorant word. "He could be one of *them*!" I stepped between them, my hands raised.

"Ma'am, he has done nothing wrong," I said loudly enough for everyone to hear. I lowered my voice to speak to her directly: "You're creating more panic than he is."

She shot daggers at me with her eyes, jaw clenched. The man glanced down at his phone. Moments later, his face fell pale as his comprehension dawned. His phone jangled, disrupting his realization. He answered, speaking rapidly in Arabic. Tears streamed down his face as it contorted itself into painful sobs.

Two hours passed. The captain authorized meal service, so we heated the breakfast meant for the flight: scrambled eggs and fruit. Passengers thanked us, staring blankly at their trays without eating. The woman in 14C hadn't stopped dialing. Each time she was unable to reach her contacts, she released another wave of fresh tears.

When we finally crept slowly toward our gate three hours later, O'Hare looked frozen in time, like a museum after it had closed. Its corridors were strangely empty in every direction. Every gate seat was vacant and every terminal abandoned.

As our group of attendants slow-walked the hallways, our footsteps echoed in the silence. We looked at each other in shock, trying to piece together what had happened. The empty airport made me feel like we had touched down as survivors, staring at the end of the world.

In a friend's car driving home, the radio filled in the gaps. "Both of the Twin Towers have collapsed…" None of the news coverage felt real or even possible.

Back at Tammy's apartment, we huddled together around the TV, glued to the horrific footage playing on an endless loop, on every channel. We were desperate to find out if all of our friends flying that day had made it home safely.

Every time we picked up the phone, the line was busy. Hundreds of us were strewn all over the country, stranded at small airports that were the closest and safest places for planes to land. Tammy and I were lucky that our flight had never left the ground.

How did it take only one moment to destroy the last vestiges of our innocence?

I watched, transfixed, as the towers collapsed over and over on the television in slow motion like sandcastles on the shore. Nothing was fair about people running through heaving clouds of debris and struggling to breathe. None of this was fair.

Three days later, I lingered in the crew room at O'Hare, staring at the Des Moines flight manifest as I leaned on the counter. Out of the 400 passengers booked, 22 had shown up. Passenger seat assignments were scattered across the 737's cabin. Even fewer passengers filled the plane on its return flight. The cockpit had once been my favorite place to hang out and chat. Now, there stood the door, locked permanently with new dead-bolts and bars.

My furlough notice arrived two weeks later. "Due to reduced passenger demand…" it began. I didn't finish reading the letter. All around me, my friends were preemptively packing up their crash pads, all of us feeling like our wings had been clipped.

I dialed Jeff's number, the phone shaking slightly in my hand.

"Can I come back to Las Vegas? Can I—go back to school?"

He answered without hesitation: "Of course you can. Come home."

8. KARISSA

WHEN I MOVED BACK IN WITH JEFF AND JULIE, WHO HAD RETURNED to Las Vegas, I immediately got to work sorting out my schooling. I was re-admitted to UNLV, and this time I was serious about finishing.

I started with a full-time course load, anxious to take on all that I could without my will to study fizzling out too quickly. In taking on such a heavy academic load, I toed the line between overachiever and certifiably insane person.

My first week back, I took a chance on attending a singles ward activity. Part of my motivation for going was the setting itself: lots of good-looking single people mingling with each other at a dry lakebed outside of Las Vegas. I introduced myself to several women with a good-natured attitude and willingness to meet as many people as I could. I hadn't anticipated recognizing anyone there.

As I wrapped up a surface-level conversation with an attractive early education major, I noticed a familiar face peering at me over a crowd that had gathered around the refreshments. There stood Karissa, the young woman I met several years before when I first attended UNLV. She had blossomed from a bright, 17-year-old girl to a confident, luminous and strikingly beautiful woman in her early 20s.

We conversed for a few minutes, catching each other up on our lives. Karissa must have found me to be an excellent listener, actively engaged in everything she was saying. Meanwhile, I internally chided myself throughout our conversation to stop staring like a fool at her soft, full lips as she spoke.

I was overjoyed to fully jump back into my life at church, especially in an all-singles ward. I moved in with Julie's brother, Steve, who was like a brother to me. We had a great time watching BYU sports since he was a graduate of BYU, basketball remaining one of my favorite activities to watch and to play with friends. I couldn't help but feel excited, too, when I noticed that Karissa started coming to our same ward.

In my new grounded life, I got a job as a bank teller for Bank of America, because they offered tuition reimbursement. Six months into my new employment, my supervisor liked my work ethic and attitude so much that I was promoted to personal banker. I excelled as a banker for an entire year before I was promoted again to branch manager. I would eventually become the consumer market manager after two short years.

Karissa became a permanent fixture in my friend group. Wayne joined, as well. A few of our friends, including Wayne and Karissa, decided to travel to Africa. I wasn't in a situation where I could afford to go, so while they were on their trip, Wayne asked me to stay at his house. A couple of days after they returned, Wayne noticed I had accidentally left one of my shirts in the closet, which he joked was a sign that I should definitely move in with him for good.

In no time at all, Wayne, Karissa and our two other mutual friends, Shane and Megan, became great friends. One of our favorite things to do was to travel together. In what would become such a pivotal time for me becoming a self-sufficient adult, Wayne was my rock. We became roommates and best friends. His generosity of spirit inspires me to this day.

———

I never once thought I was eligible to fall in love in my lifetime. For starters, I considered romantic love a luxury afforded only to people with good parents, sumptuous wardrobes and disposable incomes.

In spite of my skewed thinking—and without my express permission—the attraction I felt toward Karissa evolved all the same into a full-blown crush. I did my best to keep my feelings at bay, mostly for the sake of keeping our friendship intact.

Karissa had friends from every corner of the country, starting on campus. I never saw her alone for a minute. People were immediately drawn into her orbit because she was kind and respectful, unafraid to take chances on meeting different types of people. I admired how driven she was about schoolwork and future plans; I was still unraveling all the bad habits I had accrued while in survival mode.

Part of her five-year plan involved moving across the country. She taught at UNLV while getting her master's degree in organizational communication, assuming she would eventually get her PhD in Washington D.C., and become a professor for her career.

Our academic interests and ambitions differed, but our worlds collided nonetheless: some of the tellers I supervised during the day were students Karissa taught. Hilariously, I was 30 years old, taking the same classes as my tellers at night to earn my degree—so I made sure not to take Karissa's class.

The first time I acted on my feelings for Karissa was over Thanksgiving.

She decided not to travel back home to Idaho, so she would be staying in Las Vegas like me. She planned to have a chill weekend, preparing for finals and relaxing if possible. I opted not to travel to see family because, well, they were my family. On an impulse, I called her on Thanksgiving Day and invited her to see the latest *Harry Potter* movie with me. She agreed to come, and I went into the theater with the makings of a solid plan.

There was a scene with a jump scare that startled her, so much so that her immediate reaction was to reach for my hand to grab the closest thing she could use as a safety blanket. While a cute and otherwise normal thing to do as friends, I leveraged it as an opportunity to show my deeper feelings—I didn't let go. I remember stealing glances at her face, made even more beautiful by the light of the silver screen. She seemed at ease and completely at home with our intertwined hands. I felt relieved and wondered what took me so long.

For the next few weeks, I kept my cool around Karissa. I did not betray any more emotions if I could help it. She didn't say anything, which reassured me we had some kind of tacit agreement between us.

That year Keenan and Rebekeh invited me to spend Christmas and New Year's with them in Chicago. With their permission, I invited our friend group to come for New Year's, but only Karissa and my brother Ben could make it.

After a delicious dinner at Navy Pier, we looked for a good place to countdown to midnight and watch the fireworks over the water. In the cold, Karissa and I held hands in my jacket pocket to keep them warm. I suppressed the urge to kiss her right then and there, knowing midnight was still hours away, but I wanted our first kiss to be something I made happen with a grand gesture.

"Three, Two, One...*Happy New Year!*" I leaned in to peck Karissa on the lips. She smiled at me, then averted her eyes. Before she had the chance to say anything, I pulled her closer and kissed her again, but this time, I did not hold back. She seemed stunned.

Then she kissed me back. And we fell madly in love.

We both knew time was not on our side. Karissa had a plan, and the next step involved her moving across the country. She was elated when she got her acceptance letter to attend the PhD program at the University of Maryland outside of Washington, D.C. where she planned to pursue her doctorate.

I was teetering on the edge of a major panic attack every time I thought about spending any length of time without her. But I needed her to know that my love for her was unconditional. I made it very clear that she did not have to choose between being with me and D.C. I would follow her to the ends of the earth if I had to.

———

Karissa and I get married in the San Diego temple, then honeymoon in Asia. Our partnership is everything I once thought was just beyond my reach. When the spirit moves me, I'll interrupt her mid-story just to hug her—to remind myself she's real. All of our ambitions and pursuits align in a way that allows us to be equal partners side by side, even in business.

But first, I graduate.

It has taken me 10 years to earn my bachelor's degree in business administration, and every inch of the journey feels earned. I work full-time during the day and take classes at night. I study in parking lots, on lunch breaks and sometimes at red lights. Karissa reads my notes aloud while I drive to campus at night to take tests, focusing on key terms in the margins of textbooks. I go from memorizing the alphabet backward to writing final papers under deadlines.

On graduation day, I put on the robe—the same kind I once believed belonged only to other people, people whose parents made them breakfast before school, who rode the school bus without fear, who were expected to succeed.

I am not supposed to be here. But I am.

For a moment, I let myself feel proud. I think about hiding behind bushes as the school bus passed our house. I think about the days I pretended to study workbooks at the kitchen table, the seminary books I glued together, the moments I pretended to know how to read. I think about walking into a college class-room for the first time—a full-grown adult pretending not to be terrified.

Now I am graduating from college.

My parents attend the ceremony—something I'm grateful for, even as I brace for impact. My father comments that the graduation cap and gown look "Satanic." I tune him out. I've learned to protect my joy from my parents, who can't recognize it.

We return to our new house for an early dinner. My father and I talk about the shrinking list of things we have in common. My mother moves through the kitchen like a scavenger, opening every cupboard, silently inventorying what we've stored for the End Times. Karissa sets the table, plates in hand, when my mother turns and fires off her opinion like a shot across the bow: "You know, if you didn't eat food with high fructose corn syrup, you would probably get pregnant pretty easily."

The moment stings Karissa, but it doesn't shake me. Not the way it once would have.

I've already won.

A word about food and cooking: Karissa is from Idaho, just like my mother. Naturally, she assumed it was impossible for anyone from Idaho to mess up potatoes. And then there's Coene —exceptional in every way.

My mother has a unique approach to mashed potatoes. She peels and boils them, then drains just enough water to leave a puddle in the pan. She doesn't want them to be too dry, so she mashes them into something that more closely resembles a liquid than a solid. Butter? Salt? Sour cream? Never. The result is neither appealing nor edible.

When I was a kid, our choices were limited to being incredibly hungry or slightly nauseated by most of the food we did have. Aside from the occasional elk stew, we had turkey for Easter, Thanksgiving and Christmas—usually thanks to a food assistance program in Vernal that gave my parents one because of our family size.

We owned chickens, but only for their eggs, which were reserved for breadmaking. We had goats and rabbits, but those were for breeding and selling—we were never allowed to eat them. Our father permitted us two meals a day, no more, no less. Breakfast was oatmeal, toast or canned fruit. Dinner was vegetables and potatoes. Ben and I occasionally hid food if there was ever a surplus—something so rare we treated it like a blessing.

At our first traditional Thanksgiving as a couple, Karissa and I visited my family. She took one bite of the mashed potatoes and promptly, discreetly, spit them into a napkin. Once we were back in the car, we drove to our hotel in Vernal—but not before stopping at McDonald's for a hamburger. Karissa doesn't even like fast food, but neither of us were in a place to be choosy.

Karissa has forgiven Coene for her food-shaming and her crimes against potatoes.

Ed traveled all over the world working as a merchant marine, attending church whenever he was in port. In his late 20s, he was in St. Petersburg, Russia, where he was surprised to be able to participate in a service. The LDS church in Russia at the time did not have the authority to preach actively, but there were still some members of the church living there, most of whom were expats.

It was in St. Petersburg that Ed first met Kalijah. To this day, her background remains mysterious to us. She joined the church in 1991 after the Tabernacle Choir visited Moscow for the first time. She is a polyglot who happens to be fluent in English. The story she told is that her parents disowned her once she joined the Mormon church. I cannot confirm her story's veracity, especially considering she and Ed would visit her family in Russia years later.

Kalijah is Kyrgyz from Kyrgyzstan—most people speculate about her origin. She and Ed fell in love quickly, their early relationship consisting of cost-prohibitive long distance phone calls coordinated over different time zones and cultures. They traveled to meet each other at the temple in Stockholm, Sweden, where they planned to be wed. My parents swooned over the idea of Ed marrying a woman with such an exotic background. They bargained that she would be a modern Mormon pioneer, someone who would convert souls in Russia. But those plans and designs failed to transpire once Kalijah got to LaPoint.

After they were married at the temple in Sweden, she qualified to be a US citizen, and our mother helped buy them a trailer in LaPoint. They seemed happy for a time, then Kalijah became unglued. It might be comical to recall how she butted heads with Mom, if only it weren't so completely off base and unhinged.

Kalijah soured on LaPoint after a few months. I'm not sure exactly where they moved afterward, but they ended up in Hawaii eventually. They abandoned their trailer, leaving it in Mom's hands to sell herself. At one point, Kalijah called our mother to accuse her of purposely delaying the sale to hold onto "my Ed," as she referred to him.

In my late 20s, I joined Keenan and Rebekeh in Hawaii for their daughter's first birthday. I thought it would be great to visit Ed and Kalijah while I was there.

Things started off as normal as they ever had, all of us sitting and talking to catch each other up on our lives. Out of nowhere, Kalijah asked to talk in private. She motioned for me to join her outside, where she erupted in a stream of hateful assertions hurled at me in broken English.

She claimed I had been a terrible brother to Ed, a fact so painfully ironic I thought for a second she might be joking. The specifics she mentioned were lost in her loathsome bile. She claimed that I—as a seven-year-old child—had caused Ed tremendous pain as a 14-year-old. She alleged I formed some kind of coup against Ed with my other brothers. I stood there in shock, unsure of how to counter her false narrative. This did not seem like the right time to inform her that it had been Ed, not me, who had abused me in ways I will not elaborate on here.

I wondered if Ed had hardened her against me because of his own guilt for how he treated me growing up. He never seemed to have clued her in on how he tormented me and caused me so much pain. Her angry tirade reached its crescendo when she told me I was not welcome in their home ever again, and that it was time for me to leave.

Years later, I was married to Karissa and working as a Consumer Market Manager for Bank of America. One afternoon, I was doing branch visits with my boss—the Market Executive over all of Las Vegas—when I noticed Kalijah's name lighting up my phone.

I froze.

I hadn't spoken to her in years. Not since the visit to Hawaii when she told me I was no longer welcome in their lives or their home. I turned to my boss and said, "It's my sister-in-law in Hawaii. She never calls—I should probably make sure everything's okay."

Ed still worked on oil tankers, sailing across the world, so I assumed the worst. I stepped aside and answered the call, bracing for bad news.

Instead, I was met with a barrage of angry, broken-English shouting. "Tell wife stop calling!" she snapped.

I blinked, confused. Karissa didn't even have Kalijah's phone number.

"She call at four o'clock in morning!" Kalijah screamed. "If she not have what do at four o'clock in morning, find job to her!"

And then she hung up.

I stared at the screen, stunned. My boss looked at me, concerned. "Everything okay?" I nodded, forcing a smile. "Yeah, it's fine."

Later, I asked Karissa if she had tried to call her. She laughed. Of course not. Karissa didn't even have her number. We never figured out what that call was really about. Maybe Kalijah was confused by a telemarketer. Maybe it was misdirected rage. Maybe it was just Kalijah being Kalijah.

Fast-forward 15 years, and somehow Ed and Kalijah ended up in Las Vegas—living just a few miles from our home.

One day, I pulled up to a red light in my truck. I was in the left-turn lane, sitting high above the traffic. Across the intersection, in the opposite turn lane, I spotted a silver Honda Accord. In it sat Ed and Kalijah. They were talking, animated—arguing about something, it seemed.

I sat there, watching them through the windshield, unsure if they would notice me.

The light turned green. We both made our left turns, passing one another like ghosts—each heading in opposite directions. Living separate lives, just a few miles apart.

Two people who shared blood and history—and absolutely nothing else.

In 2009, Karissa and I had been married for three years and were living in California amid a house remodel. Ironically, our renovation crew consisted mostly of Guatemalan workers who questioned our sanity when we told them about our upcoming trip to their country of origin.

"Why would you go down there?" they asked, having just made the dangerous journey north themselves.

Our travel group consisted of five people: Karissa and me as the married couple and three single friends—my best friend Wayne, our friend Megan and my brother Ben. Our first major destination was Tikal, a place that exceeded every expectation. There was a raw, mystical quality that transported us through time. The jungle canopy created a living cathedral, filled with the screams of howler monkeys—small creatures that sounded more like jaguars, ready to devour us in the wilderness.

Seven ancient temples rose from this green maze and visitors were permitted to climb one of them. Standing atop that colossal stone structure, seeing the other six temples arranged like ancient guardians, created an overwhelming sense of connection to the civilization that flourished here millennia ago.

From Tikal, we traveled to Lake Atitlán, a place that many believe holds significance in Mormon geography. Some scholars theorize that this pristine blue lake, surrounded by towering volcanoes, could be the "Waters of Mormon" mentioned in the sacred text. Religious text and theories aside, the lake's beauty was undeniable—a perfect blue mirror reflecting volcanic peaks. I felt at once connected to nature and utterly insignificant in the face of geological machinations.

We explored Antigua, the jewel of Guatemala's colonial architecture. Antigua is just outside of Guatemala City, combining old European charm with the dramatic backdrop of active volcanoes. We hiked one of the volcanic peaks, reaching a spot where geothermal heat escapes through rocky vents. We roasted marshmallows over these natural furnaces—an experience that became even more sobering when the same volcano erupted just two weeks later, claiming several lives.

The centerpiece of our Guatemalan adventure, of course, was Jeff's third wedding to Gloria, a woman who also has a stage name I won't mention. The ceremony took place in a poor coastal town near the Belize border, a setting that would prove as memorable as it was surreal.

Our parents had flown down for the occasion, along with Ed and Kalijah. Jeff had also flown down Gloria's bridesmaids—and more accurately, her coworkers from Las Vegas.

The wedding ceremony unfolded on the beach with all of us seated, waiting contentedly for things to start. Gloria approached the shore by boat, but instead of a ceremonial procession, she greeted us with her voice carrying loudly across the water. The boat meandered around the pier before backing away, and suddenly a little girl came running out, scattering rose petals across the beach. The venue had forgotten this crucial detail and Gloria refused to make her entrance without the proper floral carpet.

She took her time to disembark from the boat. Gloria wore a white wedding dress—the most conservative way to describe the fashion we saw—with a long train trailing behind her. The triangle halter top and shorts peeking underneath her veil left little to the imagination. None of us knew how to react, except to smile and sit patiently.

The priest appeared minutes later, clearly intoxicated, slurring his words as he launched into a rambling discourse about the sanctity of marriage, emphasizing how people should marry only once and remain faithful forever.

Given that this was to be Jeff's third marriage, I wondered how much the priest knew about the people he was marrying. When he asked for a show of hands from those who had only been married to one person, only my parents, Karissa, and I could raise our hands. After what felt like too long, the priest pronounced Jeff and Gloria married, and they walked away together to board their boat, ready for the reception that proved to be equally theatrical.

We gathered at a beautifully maintained property featuring the facade of an old church, like something from *The Count of Monte Cristo*. The setting was stunning: manicured green lawns surrounding the preserved church front, with a rustic quality. Despite being in a developing nation, the venue had a timeless and ethereal beauty.

As we waited for the newlyweds' arrival, the bridesmaids emerged having nailed their colors to the mast, so to speak. Their outfits were more like nautical-themed costumes, each one of them festooned with garish white and blue—or more accurately, covered with colorful cloth napkins—all designed to show maximum cleavage and leg, paired with clear stiletto heels, their literal work shoes. They pranced around excitedly, thrilled that their friend was marrying an apparently wealthy man.

As Gloria and Jeff's boat approached the facade, fireworks exploded from behind the old church wall, arcing over our heads in an opulent display. It was genuinely impressive, though the extravagance felt jarring given Gloria's family's modest circumstances.

The excess seemed designed to showcase Jeff's wealth he has

accumulated from building auto body shops rather than to cele-brate their union.

Each reception table featured an enormous bottle of Grey Goose vodka as a centerpiece, though notably, almost no one was drinking. Gloria's parents, whom I spoke with in Spanish, were deeply religious and abstained from alcohol entirely.

As LDS members, we didn't drink, either. The bridesmaids indulged somewhat, though the atmosphere remained surpris-ingly subdued despite the lavish presentation.

The evening's most memorable moment came during the couple's first dance. After the traditional father-daughter and mother-son dances, Jeff and Gloria took the floor for what they had rehearsed as their signature moment. Gloria wrapped her leg around Jeff's waist, threw herself backward with her long black hair flying behind her, and held on with one hand while maintaining the leg lock—essentially performing what I'd venture to say was strip club choreography, with Jeff as the human-equivalent of a stabilizing pole.

My mother, watching this graphic, overtly sexual display, gazed at the couple with total curiosity and reverence: "This is interesting. This must be a cultural dance—you know, Guatemalan culture," she mused. Watching her watching Jeff and Gloria is the second funniest thing I've ever seen, after my father's multi-ply spiritual wiping tutorial.

Wayne and I couldn't contain ourselves. Here was my extremely conservative Mormon mother, for whom sex had always been the most taboo of subjects, enjoying what was effec-tively an erotic performance because she'd assumed it was "cul-tural." She couldn't see it as provocative, only provincial.

The entire wedding felt like Jeff's attempt to impress our parents—to prove his success and demonstrate his ability to provide extravagant experiences for the rest of us. This dynamic —adult children still seeking parental approval—was something Karissa often pointed out about my brothers and me specifically. The wedding perfectly captured that contradiction: Jeff staging an elaborate, expensive celebration while marrying someone our parents would never fully approve of, in circumstances that highlighted rather than concealed the unconventional nature of their relationship.

Yet there we were, enjoying ourselves.

Almost as quickly as they married, they divorced.

Just a few months later, I was serving as a bishop's counselor at church, sitting in a ward council meeting, when I received an urgent call from a friend: there had been a disturbance at Jeff's house—he had been attacked by his new girlfriend.

When I rushed over, I found his Tahoe SUV crashed through the living room wall, with a trail of blood drops leading from the front door to where his motorcycle had been parked.

Jeff, meanwhile, was texting me photos of the sunrise from Oceanside, California—acting as if nothing significant had happened and chiding me for making "a big deal out of everything."

The Guatemala wedding, in retrospect, was a perfect metaphor for Jeff's approach to life: extravagant and dramatic, leaving the rest of us to wonder what would happen next in his ongoing saga.

Or to paraphrase Paul in Corinthians: *there but by the grace of God go I.*

Karissa and I place the last box into the U-Haul, the back of which is completely stuffed and stacked with our belongings almost like a Tetris game. The sun is already beating down on us at 7 am. We are hopeful yet anxious about our latest relocation to California. Another promotion, another move—the third in five years.

My new manager greets me on my first day by sliding a stack of reports across his desk toward me. No pomp or circumstance, only immediate and urgent work. The reorganization memo arrives on a Tuesday and by Friday, half my department is gone. I find myself doing the work of three people while my supervisor takes credit for our improved sales numbers in the monthly reports.

At home, Karissa is recovering—again—from another round of procedures related to her endometriosis and infertility. Her calendar has become a roadmap of appointments, medications, and hard-earned hope. She tracks everything—doctor visits, hormone levels, injection sites, side effects—with clinical precision.

Some of the procedures have names I can barely pronounce: Laparoscopic cystectomy—scraping away ovarian cysts. Hysterosalpingogram—injecting dye into her fallopian tubes. Sonohysterogram—inflating a balloon in her cervix to check the uterine cavity.

Each treatment comes with a new set of medications. Karissa struggles with every pill and injection. "I don't feel right when I take this," she says, her frustration as much about what she's losing as what she's chasing. She tries not to hate her body for what it won't do. She tries not to cry when she looks in the mirror. But she continues—because all of this might lead to the baby we've both been praying for.

Her upper arms are covered in deep purple and fading yellow bruises, each one like a phase of the moon. Every blood test reveals a new imbalance, a new dosage adjustment, a new round of side effects. Her hormone levels swing back and forth like a pendulum with no center.

And then there are the needles.

Karissa is terrified of them. She passes out so often during blood draws that they've stopped trying to have her sit upright. They lay her flat in a bed, and if she faints—she usually does—they hold ammonia under her nose and keep going.

It's routine now. She braces for the embarrassment before it even begins, apologizing to every new phlebotomist who doesn't know her pattern yet.

And still, she shows up. Over and over again.

We try, month after month, to conceive.

My molar cracks on a weekday morning, the crown splitting against my tongue. I taste copper and sigh.

"I need to see a dentist," I told my boss.

"No, you don't. Not until the executive visit is done," he replied.

For 21 days, I chewed on one side of my mouth, washing down ibuprofen with soda. By the time I finally sat in the dentist's chair, she shook her head. "Your gums have receded permanently. We'll need to do extensive work."

The executive never came to our branch locations. My boss used this as an excuse to evaluate my performance.

I'm almost ready to type my resignation letter.

I knew Jeff's son, Terry, from the day he was born. I was his favorite uncle, and we shared a bond that ran deep. When he was 12, Jeff was granted full custody of him after a series of poor choices by Jeff's ex-wife Crystal. For a time, I lived with Jeff and Julie while Terry was there, too. Later, when Jeff and Julie divorced, Jeff and Terry came to live with Karissa and me while they rebuilt their lives.

Years later, we traveled to Las Vegas for Christmas and found that Terry had nowhere to go for the holidays. He was living in a seedy, pay-by-the-week motel and had clearly hit rock bottom. Karissa and I invited him to spend Christmas with us. We were grateful to see him, but the more he shared about his situation, the bleaker his circumstances seemed. He admitted he was selling drugs on the Strip for a local gangster who lived in his building.

Things had gotten so bad that Jeff had allegedly cut him off financially. We decided to offer Terry a chance to make a clean break from Vegas.

He was about to turn nineteen but hadn't yet finished high school. We wanted to help him reset—to empower him to complete his education and start making better choices. We invited him to come live with us in California, where we had recently moved for my promotion. We laid out clear conditions:

First, he had to cut ties with the friends who were dragging him down and get rid of his phone. Second, he had to commit to a church-based 12-step addiction recovery program. Third, he had to earn his high school diploma.

Terry agreed. And for a few months, it looked like the arrangement might actually work. He was fun to have around—boisterous, full of energy and always charismatic.

But once he got a job, things started to unravel. He gravitated back toward the same types of people and habits he'd promised to leave behind.

While Karissa and I were away in Guatemala for Jeff's wedding to Gloria, we left Terry in the house. The trip lasted 10 days. When we returned, it took only seconds to realize something had gone horribly wrong. The house was a disaster and neighbors were complaining about loud parties. Inside, we found bent spoons with milky-white residue, lighters and half-used bottles of household chemicals scattered around the bathroom.

Terry's demeanor had changed, too. He was no longer the upbeat, eager-to-start-over version of himself. He had hardened—withdrawn, angry, volatile. And yet, in a strange way, his ability to engineer high-potency drugs from everyday materials reflected a kind of dark brilliance, creativity and ingenuity. He would have been a prolific scientist if drugs had not taken him as soon as they did.

We agreed he couldn't stay. His grandmother—Crystal's mother—came to pick him up.

Shortly after, Karissa and I traveled to Las Vegas to visit her sister, who was having a baby. The night the baby was born, we were visiting Wayne when our neighbor from California called around midnight. She said she'd seen a U-Haul parked at our house during odd hours. Suspicious, she had peered through the window—and saw the place had been completely ransacked.

We drove home immediately. By 2 am, we were standing in the ruins of our home. The burglars had taken everything: our clothes, cherished family photos, Karissa's jewelry, my mission memorabilia from Brazil. Even half-used bottles of soap and shampoo from our shower were gone.

It looked like the Grinch had come—but this time, he didn't just steal Christmas. He took everything.

As we stood together in the closet, surveying the empty hangers and blank walls, we noticed something strange. Nearly every article of Karissa's clothing was gone—hundreds of shirts, shoes and business pant-suits—except for two lonely blouses still hanging on the rod.

Karissa picked one up and held it in front of her as if trying it on, her eyes still wet with tears. "What's wrong with this shirt?" she asked, dead serious. "It's not good enough to steal?" She turned to me, broken-hearted and bewildered. "You never told me I looked stupid in this shirt!"

She started to cry—and then we both realized the comedy in her words. Suddenly we were laughing hysterically, then crying again. The burglars had stripped our lives clean, but even in the wreckage, humor had a way of sneaking in. We stood in the closet, laughing and crying at the same time, holding onto each other because there was nothing else left to hold onto.

Everything we owned was gone. But somehow, in that moment, we still had each other—and just enough humor to make it through.

We couldn't say for sure who was behind the burglary. But in our hearts, we suspected Terry.

When he slid back into rock bottom, it seemed he tried to drag us down with him.

"Medicare insurance? Really?" Karissa looked at me skeptically. "Why are you leaving a stable, well-paying job for one that pays commissions?" I appealed to her logical side with my spreadsheets and plans, so even with her doubts, she supported me.

I studied hard for three days, then took the state insurance license exam, which I passed immediately. I was ecstatic. In short order, I resigned from Bank of America.

Karissa was still worried, and understandably so. I had just walked away from a stable job in the middle of an economic crisis—the Great Recession. But once I shared my full vision with her—what I believed this could become—she was all in.

I called Wayne. "Hey," I said casually, "did you happen to notice if I left a shirt in the closet?" That was our code. It meant: We're moving in. He understood immediately. "Come on home," he said.

Las Vegas had only ever been good to me.

And just like that, we moved in with Wayne—temporarily, but with all the humility and urgency of people starting over.

In two weeks' time, we found out Karissa was pregnant. She went to the pharmacy once it dawned on her what could be happening and she bought every type of pregnancy test there was. I'd waited eagerly outside the bathroom door trying to curb my excitement in case we were met with a negative again.

When she finally opened the door, there were tears in her eyes. I looked over at the countertop to see no less than eight tests with a combination of double lines and plus marks boldly fixed across the tests. Her tears turned into hyperventilation as she squealed, "They are all positive! All of them! Look!"

Despite the fact that we had lost all of our belongings in the home invasion and I had just quit my job, we were pregnant. We held each other for a long embrace, letting all of the tears flow. This would be us starting from scratch and we couldn't be happier.

A few months later during an ultrasound scan, we learned we were having a boy. My mind instantly flashed all the way back to the father and son I had seen while in Brazil over 15 years earlier. I couldn't believe I was finally going to become a father, something I had desired for so long.

When I started my first company, Karissa wasn't initially involved. It was the same year she became pregnant with our son, Christian. But with her background—including graduate studies in organizational communication—she quickly proved invaluable. While she organized playdates, led mom groups and threw themed birthday parties at home, the business began to grow. And eventually, it needed more help.

Karissa's sister stepped in to help with Christian so Karissa could begin coming into the office a few days a week. She started answering phones, building spreadsheets, managing the calendar—essentially running the front desk. She joked that it was beneath her pay grade, but we both knew: we were in this together. We would do whatever it took to make it work.

As the company grew and we hired our first agents, Karissa's role expanded. When our daughter, Victoria, was born five years later—prematurely, in a terrifying medical whirlwind—Karissa stepped away for three months to care for both of our children. Then, without fanfare or complaint, she came right back to work, managing multiple people without ever drawing a paycheck.

For years, we reinvested every dollar we earned back into the company. We lived frugally because we believed in what we were building.

And our sacrifices paid off.

The turning point—the thing that set us apart—was simple but groundbreaking: we reimagined how a Medicare agency could operate. We built a business called The Medicare Store, where independent agents became part of a true team. It might sound cliché, but we turned Medicare into a team sport. Our agents weren't competing—they were collaborating. Together, they upheld high standards, shared in the success of unified marketing, and held one another accountable.

The brand quickly became recognizable—first in Las Vegas, then Reno, and eventually across Nevada, Texas, New Mexico and Arizona. At The Medicare Store, clients aren't left waiting on a single agent to return their call. They have access to our full Service Excellence Team—people who call, text and check in proactively. That level of care costs more, but the value it delivers is undeniable. Our clients feel supported, understood and well taken care of. They refer friends and family without us even asking.

What made this model thrive—and what continues to guide us—is our commitment to being Agents of Change.

To us, an Agent of Change is someone who sees a problem in their community—large or small—and takes action to create meaningful, lasting change. It's not just what we do; it's who we are. That identity is built on a set of shared values that shape how we show up for each other and for our clients:

A: Absolutely Positively Gritty
- Be optimistic in the present and excited for the future
- Have passion and perseverance for long-term goals

G: Good People Doing Good Things
- Always act with integrity and do what is right
- Help people live healthy and happy lives

E: Enjoying Work and Life
- Laugh every day
- Celebrate successes

N: Noticeably Professional
- Be ready, willing and able
- Show professionalism in appearance, language and attitude

T: Team and Family
- Welcome, encourage and support each other
- Cultivate personal relationships

S: Striving for Excellence
- Continually improve and make changes when necessary
- Embrace process, solutions and technology

These aren't just slogans on a wall. Our team created them together. They weren't handed down from me—they emerged from who we already were and who we aspired to be. The Agents of Change values were born from real conversations, real experiences and a shared desire to build something meaningful. They're embedded in how we train, how we hire how we serve and how we lead.

We created a culture where agents have flexibility but are held to high standards of preparation, ethics and excellence.

Sometimes our agents spend hours helping someone, only to conclude that the best advice is to stay on their current plan. That trust-first approach is how we've grown.

We've refused to hire "sales sharks," no matter how profitable they might be. Instead, we bring on people who genuinely care—who believe that helping someone understand their options is just as valuable as making a sale. That kind of leadership multiplies. And it works.

We didn't stop there.

We created Nuvo Health as a parent company—an umbrella brand supporting independent brokers and larger teams alike. We launched Medicare Hub, a "brand in a box" that offers legitimacy, infrastructure and support to independent agents while allowing them the freedom to work under their own name or ours.

Then came PlanFit, our national call center. After COVID shifted the way people interact, we adapted quickly. PlanFit helps people across the country—no matter where they live—find the Medicare plan that fits their needs. To uphold our standards, we staffed the team with salaried agents who are paid to help, not to sell. Their job is to educate and guide, regardless of whether the person enrolls.

We also launched Nuvo Wealth—a boutique wealth management firm that's grown entirely through referrals, run by a trusted friend and guided by the same core values.

What began as one agent has become a national Medicare agency and Field Marketing Organization (FMO) with heart. Nuvo Health, with Nuvo Wealth, The Medicare Store, Medicare

Hub and PlanFit under its umbrella, is a growing force. We offer Medicare and health insurance services nationwide.

The business continues to grow—one right decision at a time. We've built it on hard work, a bit of luck (though I believe the harder I work, the luckier I get) and the quiet, persistent presence of God in the details.

But beyond the business success lies a deeper truth: this story has always been about partnership.

Karissa and I built this together.

Rather than being a barrier, my traumatic childhood made me more devoted to her than I ever thought possible. I had never truly felt love until Karissa. Her love gave me the capacity to love back—tenfold. We worked through pain, fear and uncertainty side by side.

People often say, "Behind every successful man is a supportive woman." I always correct them. Karissa has never been behind me. She has been beside me—every day, every meeting, every risk, every win.

Together, we've raised children, built a home and launched multi-million-dollar business—always grounded in the same two principles: integrity and service.

Our lives continue to expand because we trust each other, and we trust in God. We are limited only by the reach of our imaginations and the faith to keep trying.

What began as a business idea became a new approach to Medicare—one that has helped tens of thousands of people make informed decisions about their health care.

We thrive because we built something real. Something rooted in care. Something we never stop building together.

I continued to serve in various church callings, with my responsibilities increasing year after year, until I was asked to serve as the bishop of my ward, a congregation of over 400 members. It became one of the most demanding, miraculous and sacred chapters of my life.

In The Church of Jesus Christ of Latter-day Saints, bishops

are not paid clergy; we're lay leaders, called to serve for an average of five years. We don't campaign or apply for the role—most men don't even hope for it. But when I was asked to serve, I said yes.

Being a bishop is like being a pastor, a counselor, a manager and a shepherd all in one. It was a full-time spiritual job on top of everything else in my life. My responsibilities ranged from overseeing Sunday worship services and mentoring teenagers, to helping families in crisis and administering welfare assistance. I sat with people in grief and in confession. I mourned with those who mourned and rejoiced with those who found light again. I even officiated at weddings and funerals. I came to see people the way I imagine their Heavenly Father sees them.

One of the greatest privileges of that calling was working with the young men in the priests quorum. I guided them as they prepared for missions, administered the sacrament each Sunday, led quorum discussions and navigated the growing complexity of teenage life. We talked about faith, leadership, identity and what it means to live with integrity. Those boys took over part of my heart, and they still own it today. I've watched them go on missions, start families, join the military and serve in their communities. They became the kind of strong, good men the world desperately needs more of.

Serving as a bishop is both exhausting and exquisite. It stretches your capacity to love in every direction. The more I gave, the more my heart seemed to expand—like it was being fueled by something far greater than my own effort.

But, as it is with all growth, that expansion was painful.

At the same time I was caring for my spiritual flock, I was also caring for my business and family—trying to grow a business and a family in parallel. Our company was taking off at a pace that felt nothing short of miraculous. Then, after years of infertility, Karissa became pregnant with our daughter, Victoria, on what was to be our final round of intrauterine insemination.

If it hadn't worked, we had decided Christian would be our only child. Karissa's body had been through all it could take.

The pregnancy was difficult, and the delivery nearly broke me. I tremble even now when I think back to that moment—running down the hallway with doctors and nurses to the operating room—not knowing if I was about to lose my wife, my daughter or both. I was a bishop, a man of faith but in that moment, I was just a husband, praying for a miracle.

That prayer was answered. Somehow, I walked out of that hospital a week later with both of my girls.

As a bishop, my heart had never been so full. And yet, I was often completely overwhelmed. Being a bishop, a husband, a father and a business owner all at once meant carrying more than I thought I was capable of. I often went to bed spent—spiritually, emotionally, physically—praying for strength, and waking up just in time to be needed again.

It was the hardest thing I've ever done. And the holiest.

A man I've never seen at church before sits across from me in my bishop's office. I'm preparing to counsel him, but it's clear he's holding something back.

His hands tremble as he grips the arms of his chair. We've been talking in circles for hours, the wall clock ticking just past 11:30 pm. I'm uniquely qualified to spot someone lying to themselves, and my senses sharpen the more the man in front of me equivocates.

"We've been here a while," I say gently. "I can tell something's really bothering you. I think you'll feel better if you just let it out. Don't you?"

He exhales in one deep burst of air. He searches for the right words—and when he finds them, they hit like a physical blow. He begins to describe a vile act he has perpetrated on his seven-year-old daughter.

I work hard to swallow back tears and the mix of anger and bile rising in my throat.

When he finishes confessing, his eyes change. He lifts his

head and looks like a wild animal that's been cornered—or a scorpion surrounded by fire. We are alone in the building, a fact that only now starts to bother me.

"We should go," I say, keeping my voice steady.

I lock the door behind us and we walk across the parking lot. I jangle my keys nervously in my pocket, trying to make small talk while carefully sidestepping a landmine. I stall at my car—checking my phone, ready to dial 911—until I'm sure he's gone.

When I get home safely, I call the police. My voice shakes as I explain what I've heard.

The detective who takes my statement asks follow-up questions with clinical detachment. Weeks later, the only update I'm given is that a custody order has been issued, severing his parental rights. I'm stunned that he isn't arrested—and baffled when he continues showing up at church for several more weeks.

I walk around in a fatigue state, sleeping with a handgun in a biometric safe at my bedside.

During Sunday service the following week, I sit in my usual seat at the front of the chapel, facing the congregation. Suddenly, Christian bolts for the water fountain in the hallway. Seconds later, I see the same man—slowly rising from his pew, walking toward the exit on the same side of the chapel.

I make a quick plea to God as I begin to stand: *God, you've asked me to be a bishop. You have to protect my family.*

I step away from the stand, but before I reach the bottom stair, Christian reappears through the door. I return to my seat as the congregation watches me, puzzled.

For months afterward, I jump at every creak in the house. His voicemails pile up—pleas, desperate requests to meet again, "just once." I leave them unanswered until he eventually disappears from the congregation.

I never see him darken another doorway again.

But I still check around corners.

9. IN DEFENSE OF HEARTBREAK

Dad's fall happened on a cold day in early April.

He took a wrong step off of the converted garage step and toppled to the ground, breaking his hip. Most people would immediately call an ambulance when they found someone writhing in pain, crying for help on the frozen ground.

My mother "nursed" him instead. My parents don't think like most people.

Rather than call 911, Mom dialed my nephew, who lived 15 miles away. Together with a neighbor, they tried to lift Dad themselves. When that failed, they rolled him onto a board and loaded him into the back of a pickup truck, then drove him to the hospital in Vernal in the bitter cold.

The image of my elderly father in agony, bouncing in the back of a truck on a blustery night when an ambulance was just a phone call away, makes me feel physically ill. Their stubborn adherence to what they saw as self-reliance often bordered on dangerous negligence.

Mom recounted this story to me casually over the phone that night, as if it were the most natural course of action to take in the world. It was the same mindset that led them to embrace conspiracy theories about modern medicine while rejecting practical solutions that could alleviate suffering.

Given the choice between man-made medical advances and God's perceived natural cures, God won out every time.

The hip surgery went well initially, and Jeff, Ben and I went to Vernal to help during Dad's recovery. But then came the setback that would invite his final days. Dad forgot he wasn't supposed to walk unassisted and got up to use the bathroom alone, falling and breaking his femur.

I had never before seen another human being in such intense, unrelenting pain. He was writhing, crying like a child, unable to find even a moment's relief. Yet Mom, paralyzed by her fear of "playing God," had refused to authorize adequate pain medication. She was terrified that morphine would hasten his death, making her complicit in what she saw as ending his life.

"I was afraid to make that decision," she told me, tears in her eyes. "What if giving him pain medicine means he dies? That would mean I was the cause of his death." She bowed her head, ashamed.

I realized at that moment that this impossible choice couldn't rest on her shoulders alone. This was my father, and I couldn't watch him suffer when relief was readily available. I told the medical staff to administer morphine—enough to quiet his agony. Less than 12 hours later, he passed peacefully.

Later, Mom would say to me, "I hope he forgives me for not taking away his pain sooner. I just didn't know what to do." But I assured her she had made the only decision a spouse could make, and that I was grateful I could take that burden from her in his final hours.

Strangely, in his final years, as dementia softened the harder edges of his personality, Dad became someone I could almost enjoy being around. He was kinder to me, complimentary to my wife and would hug me and tell me he was proud of me. I found myself liking this version of my father in a way I never had before—as if his vituperative mind, which had been the source of so much dysfunction, had finally gotten out of the way of his heart.

The plastic slide gleamed orange with the last rays of sunlight touching us before sunset. I watched diligently as Christian scrambled up onto one step after another, his diaper crinkling with every big step he took. Once he reached the summit, he froze, tears falling easily from his concerned eyes.

"Mama!" His voice cracked on the second syllable.

I shifted against the doorframe, watching him fight to figure this puzzle out. The smell of sautéed vegetables wafted to me from where Karissa stood over the stove, wooden spoon in hand.

"MA-MA!" Christian called again, louder this time.

She turned the burner to low. Karissa's bare feet slapped against the patio as she jogged outside, wiping flour on the towel she held in her hands. She knelt beside the slide, her voice gentle and kind.

"Turn your body this way, little bug. Like this."

Her hands guided his small frame until he faced the slide, then he squealed with delight as he pushed off.

Back up he went. Same problem. Same call. Then—Click. Footsteps followed. Gentle instruction. Laughter was set adrift in the cool air.

On the fourth trip outside, Karissa's ponytail had come loose, wisps of hair sticking to her damp forehead. "You don't need to run out here every time," I said, my arms crossed. "That's just spoiling him."

Karissa's hands stilled on Christian's shoulders. She looked at me for a long moment, then walked over. Her fingers found mine and gently pulled my arms apart, placing them around her waist while she looked up at me.

"Babe." Her voice was soft but steady. "That is not spoiling him. You can't spoil a child by loving him. That—*that* is what love looks like."

My heart leaped as tears caught in my throat.

"When our children need us," she continued, her hand still clasping mine, "we will be there. That's our job. That's just love."

Behind us, Christian called out again from the top of the slide. Without hesitation, I squeezed her hand and walked toward our son.

———

Karissa wakes before me most mornings—somewhere between 5 and 5:30 am. By 6:30, she's opening shutters in the kids' rooms, letting their music play for a few precious minutes before the day officially begins.

The kitchen becomes mission control as either of us tackles breakfast and slides prepped lunches into Christian and Victoria's backpacks. When the kids tumble downstairs at 7 am, the real choreography begins—Karissa rushing around braiding Victoria's hair, hunting for missing shoes, while I lead our morning scripture study with a spiritual thought, asking questions aloud to inspire the kids to think about kindness and faith throughout their day.

Sometimes we sit at the table peacefully as a family; more often, one or more of us is racing against the clock.

Karissa says, "Sometimes our scripture study doesn't look pretty." And she's right. But, at least we're doing it. Finally, we gather around the kitchen table for family prayer, asking God to bless us with a good day—and to help us be a blessing to those in need.

By 7:20, Karissa is shuttling kids to school, then settling into her office by 8 am for a full day of work, skipping lunch so that she can wrap up at 2:30. She carefully orchestrates her afternoons of carpools and activities. Victoria pirouettes between dance, gymnastics, theater, piano and singing lessons, while Christian bounces from football to basketball to volleyball to track. I am always traveling for work, so Karissa leans on her network of carpool friends to keep everyone moving.

Dinner happens in stolen moments between activities, something quick from the crockpot or grabbed on the go. While Victoria practices gymnastics, Karissa sits in the gym's lobby fielding work calls and emails, seamlessly juggling her roles as mom and COO.

At bedtime, the family kneels together for evening prayer—they call me when I'm traveling so if I'm available, I can be part of morning and bedtime family prayer—rotating who leads as they count blessings and ask for continued blessings. We ask the kids to remember that our prayers are more like conversations with God, nothing memorized or scripted. We'll pray about people we know or specific events. Victoria thanks God for things like the roses blooming in the yard, and lately, she has been saying "Thank you for sending Jesus" while she's praying to God and it melts my heart. Christian will ask for blessings for an upcoming game or test. Karissa and I ask for the Lord to guide us as we make decisions for our companies and our family. Our prayers never fall on deaf ears.

Then comes the mommy/daughter sacred bedtime ritual: "A kiss and a hug for my little Tori bug," while Christian and I bond over playing Fortnite. Karissa ends the night sitting on Christian's bed for the day's best conversation when he opens up to his mother, the person he says can fix anything—and he's not wrong.

It's in this ordinary Tuesday living—filled with kitchen dance parties, dinner table stories about math tests and monkey bar chases—that our foundation builds itself, and the fissures in my heart heal…one small miracle at a time.

———

The phone ringing interrupted my thoughts. Before I could finish saying, "Hello?" my mother's voice came through the receiver hurriedly.

"Kate has cancer. The doctors want to fill her full of poison."

She lowers her voice into a conspiratorial whisper. "I told her about black salve. It can cure cancer, as you know."

Through the phone, I hear the sounds of Kate coughing in the next room, her husband Mike's voice drowning her out: "Kate, get those chickens fed before you lay down, will you?"

———

Kate had been eager to live closer to my mother in LaPoint, so she jumped at the opportunity to move a couple of years before she died. Kate was Mom's "favorite" child and self-proclaimed best friend. She tended to a garden that stretched behind the single-wide trailer that was her pride and joy. She created spectacular displays of tomatoes climbing makeshift trellises and sunflowers craning their stems like necks turning their faces to the sun, growing taller than the rusty fence posts beside them. She worked tirelessly to pull weeds, despite how her health declined so markedly over such a short period of time.

———

The single-wide trailer groaned under the weight of so many people. Kate's 10 children filled every corner—sprawled on the couch, sitting cross-legged on the floor, leaning against the wood-paneled walls. The air was thick with the smell of casseroles from church ladies and the underlying medicinal scent of hospice care.

I found myself squeezed between two of Kate's sons on the tiny couch, watching her daughter from New York tune a guitar in the corner. Her voice when she started to sing was Kate's voice, 30 years younger.

Kate lay in the hospital bed they'd moved into what used to be the living room, her breathing shallow but steady. When the music started, her eyes would flutter open and her lips would move slightly, as if she were singing along. She always did have an ear for a good melody.

Kate's daughter from Australia arrived with her fiancé on a Wednesday, their faces ashen with jet lag and worry. She knelt beside Kate's bed and took her mother's hand.

"Mom, we want to get married here. With you."

Kate's eyes opened—really opened—for the first time in days. Her mouth curved into something that might have been a smile.

Two days later, they wheeled Kate's bed into the center of the cramped living room. Ten adult children and their families pressed against the wood-paneled walls. Her daughter brought a special dress all the way from Australia for the occasion.

The officiant—a long-time family friend from the church in LaPoint—had to speak loudly over the hum of Kate's oxygen machine.

"Do you take this man."

Kate squeezed her daughter's hand. Her eyes were bright, focused and present in a way they hadn't been for weeks.

The kiss lasted three seconds. Kate's smile lasted until she fell asleep an hour later.

She died the next morning as the sun came up over the Uinta Mountains, her daughter's wedding flowers still fresh on the nightstand.

———

Kate is the first of my siblings to die.

As an adult, I feel myriad emotions toward all my brothers and sisters, but especially her. She always seemed at peace with herself in a way that had eluded me my entire life. All my older siblings were born at least a decade before me, so it follows they would die sooner into my adulthood. Death always could shock me but never surprises me.

It's a miracle any of us made it out of our house alive.

I do not feel prepared for her funeral. The cemetery grass is brown and brittle under the despondent December sky, and I am struggling to find words as I stand at the head of Kate's grave, a folded paper in my hand with the dedicatory prayer I'd been asked to give.

Mike stands to my left, his dress shirt too tight around his neck, almost as if someone has their hands clasped tightly around his throat. To my right, Kyle—Kate's first husband—is holding his second wife's hand and watching his children weep for the mother who'd raised them after he left.

Mom sits in a folding chair in the front row, her black coat buttoned to her chin, staring at the casket with dry eyes.

The empty seats around us speak volumes about the people who are not here. Jeff's chair sits vacant—he'd told Mom he couldn't handle another conversation about buying her a house. Ed hasn't returned my calls. September lives in Whiterocks, hardly 15 minutes away, but doesn't come because she's still angry about being asked not to enter Kate's room and instead to wait for Kate to be wheeled into the living room for a visit the week prior to her passing. When I finish the prayer, the wind picks up, scattering dried leaves across my father's headstone next to the plot where Kate will be buried.

———

After the funeral, Mom sits at her kitchen table, frowning. She has fanned her bills out on the table like a fortune teller predicting financial ruin.

"Thirty thousand dollars," she says, not looking up. "Gone."

The foreclosure notice jumps to my attention from the pile of envelopes in front of me. The single-wide that Kate had died in was already scheduled for repossession.

"Dad's life insurance money?"

Mom nods. "All of it. I thought...I thought if Kate had a place of her own, maybe..." Her voice trails off.

Through the window, I can see the empty trailer next door. Its windows are darkened, and Kate's garden is already overrun, strangled by winter weeds.

"The sewer line's backing up again," Mom says quietly. "And the roof is leaking in the bedroom."

I fold the foreclosure notice and put it back on the table. I wonder how long my mom will last here.

I can't help but feel we are both sitting in her coffin.

————

With Dad mysteriously and otherwise occupied at home and Mom working in town, Ben and I became custodians of Uvene's care when we were still young. We were her daily companions in a house that was often overtaken by September's kids running in and out of rooms. In those early years, Uvene's care meant laundering cloth diapers—mountains of them that needed hand washing, folding and changing throughout the day. What started as my older sisters' responsibility gradually became mine as they grew up and moved on with their lives. In their wake, Ben and I were left to wrestle with safety pins and soggy cotton while trying not to breathe through our noses.

But the mornings were different.

Those were the times when Ben and I would help Uvene, our perfect sister with Down syndrome, get ready for the day, and somehow the routine became something gentle and loving between us. I learned to work a brush through her hair without pulling too hard, to gather it into ponytails that wouldn't slide out by lunchtime. My hands grew steady with practice. I learned to hold bobby pins between my teeth while I wrapped sections around the curling iron, counting to ten before releasing each curl.

On Sundays, Mom had us get Uvene ready for church. I'd braid her hair, my fingers moving through the familiar motions without thinking until it lay neat and smooth down her back.

Those mornings spent learning to plait and pin curls were a

gift to me. When I became the father of a baby girl, I felt prepared. I can make my seven-year-old daughter feel like Elsa the Ice Queen. That practical display of love convinces me I've become the father to her that I always wanted and needed as a child.

————

The best part of my days was coming home to Uvene's voice calling from wherever she was in the house: "Calvin! How ya doin'?"

It didn't matter if I'd had the worst day at work or if I was in a bad mood, her enthusiasm never wavered. She'd wrap her arms around me like I'd been gone for months instead of hours, and somehow the day's frustrations evaporated in those small moments.

Thirty years later, that greeting hasn't changed. I sometimes visit Uvene, where she is living with our mother in a small and cramped trailer. She busies herself by playing with her stuffed animals and watching her favorite Disney movies. In so many ways, she is locked in her childhood eternally, like a jewel permanently suspended in resin. Yet she is more free than any of us will ever hope to be.

Regardless of how long I've been away, she appears with the same happy greeting: "Calvin! How ya doin'?" The tenderness I feel in my heart for Uvene is such a singular part of my emotional world because of how her innocence—and to some degree, mine—are inextricably bound and preserved with time.

Uvene does not seem to carry the same trauma the rest of us do—as if it is simply not part of her DNA.

Our family has grown large over the years: nine kids, nearly 30 grandchildren, names and faces and birthdays that even I struggle to keep straight. But Uvene knows them all. Every single one. She carries our entire family tree in her heart, each person's name ready to greet warmly, each relationship treasured and remembered.

She has never once looked at her parents or siblings with scorn or held resentment over the years. Every day her memory is wiped clean, pure as the driven snow. She has always been our family's keeper of joy because she is the only one who can make room for all of us. She shelters our happiness as only she can— Uvene, our most faithful.

The people who taught me how to love—my wife Karissa, my best friend Wayne, my former colleague Tammy, my friend Keenan—became my true family. Not because my siblings aren't important, but because these are the people who consistently showed up for me, who taught me through their example what healthy relationships could look like.

They met me where I was—and they loved me, anyway.

Wayne, who shares my appreciation for dysfunctional family stories and has become more of a brother to me than my biological brothers, lives in Phoenix now, which is close enough for us to see each other regularly. Tammy, who had been a better sister to me than my actual sisters, had the emotional capacity to do so. My chosen family members filled the gaps left by my childhood and showed me what was possible.

People often ask me how or why I am still part of the LDS faith.

I know it is easy to conflate how my parents practiced their extreme version of Mormonism with the church itself, but that is a gross oversimplification of something that is far too complex to distill into a binary.

What I am in the process of doing—and have been since I was on my mission in Brazil—is to experience the "deconstruction"[5] of my childhood religious upbringing. It has been a painful process of redefining my faith through lived experiences and my relationship with God. Our faith is the cornerstone of life for our family, and I believe our relationships with each other are richer and have more depth because of it. I'm not sure if I would be able to show up as the father and husband I am today if it weren't for the teachings of the church that have been so integral in my ability to forgive.

———

Memory is a funny thing. A dozen people can experience the same reality, yet each of them forms a different memory or perspective. A friend of mine explained to me that whenever we recall something or a memory flash in our minds, our brains are just remembering *the last time we remembered* or recalled that same memory. Some events are so significant that certain smells or words, even notes in a song, can set us on a collision course with old feelings, long buried. Other people in my life likely remember the same events I do, but we processed them very differently along the way. The one thing we usually agree on is the feeling and result of what happened. We are all damaged and most of us have been either hiding or overcompensating ever since.

There came a point a few years ago when I realized that I felt broken and somehow incomplete inside. I knew that my day of reckoning with my past was imminent, but I had never taken the time to ask myself if I was getting what I needed as a person.

Money was not the solution. It allowed for travel and the enjoyment of many good things in my life, but I often struggled to stay in the moment. I was constantly looking for more and never satisfied, at least at times when I was under enormous, mostly self-imposed stress.

When I looked in the mirror, I still saw that little boy whose idea of self was so fragmented—a different part of me reflected back in each of the broken shards of the mirror behind my parents' bedroom door. I still saw myself as unlovable. Except now, I'm an adult nearing a half-century old with no better sense of how to love myself than when I started.

And so, I began to listen more carefully to someone I admire a great deal: Joe Polish, founder of Genius Network and Genius Recovery. He speaks a lot about addiction and how behaviors manifest themselves in all sorts of ways, all stemming from the same source: pain. He speaks frankly about how to access the pain within ourselves by confronting those thoughts or deeply held beliefs that still sting when we touch them. He urges us to consider that addiction is not a separate phenomenon that we need to malign; it's our way of coping with things that are so much bigger than us. Whether it's drugs, alcohol, work, sex—whatever—it's all about trying to escape that pain, even if the relief is temporary.

"The real question isn't, 'Why the addiction?' it's 'Why the pain?'" as the renowned Hungarian Canadian physician Gabor Maté says.

I've thought about this a lot over the years. Addiction is just about the least effective solution to any real problem. Addictive behaviors might numb you in the moment when you feel pain most acutely, which seems like the only way to cope. But addiction thrives and grows in isolation.

Connection—not numbness or loneliness—is the true antidote to addiction.

I have come to realize that part of my breaking free from control and isolation is to let others in. Connecting with other people is both terrifying and exhilarating, somehow both happening at the same time. My challenge is to seek out relationships I once assumed were out of reach. My default has always been to remain emotionally isolated for most of my life. Breaking free meant forgiving those who hurt me most. Anger can be a useful emotion at times, but for me, it is a caustic thing to hold inside. I've learned to accept people with their limits, just as I have learned to accept mine.

———

Many in my family, like my nephew, Terry—who passed away from a Fentanyl overdose—search for temporary solutions for their pain. For me, the only solution that has ever worked is trusting and relying on God.

There are times when I've felt Him guiding me, then there are other times when I have felt genuine fear of God. It has taken me years to see that my addiction has always been my drive to succeed. But with every one of my successes, I have had a mentor help me see that my drive had a distinctive source: a deep well of pain.

Earlier in my career, I would have told you that I was driving so hard because I wanted to be happy and to have a great life for me and my family. But the truth is, my spirit was seared with pain from the notion that I was not, and never would be, good enough.

I thought my life's work was to catch up to everyone else, to be normal. If there is something that I've internalized the most from Dan Sullivan and Strategic Coach, it's that now I want to do what I enjoy doing because it falls within my unique abilities.

I have the courage to do things out of love, not because of pain or fear. The rewards for my success are secondary to the knowledge that I am creating and moving in a way that is authentic to who I am at my core.

The demons are still there—the capacity for rage, the old patterns of thinking, the wounds that haven't fully healed, if they ever will. But now, I have tools to work with, people who love me despite my deficiencies, and most importantly the awareness to observe my shortcomings without being controlled by them.

Even with a beautiful family and successful life, I still wrestle with the demons inherited from my childhood. Just recently, I lost my temper with Christian over something minor—his mild disrespect toward his mother triggered something in me that felt disproportionate and familiar.

But here's what's different now: I recognize it.

I feel the heat rising, observe the anger as it happens and can step back from it. After cooling down, I went to Christian's room and offered him something I never received as a child—a genuine apology without conditions or emotional manipulation.

"I realize I was wrong," I told him. "I shouldn't have lost my temper, and I'm asking for your forgiveness." I explained that I was learning to see him as the young adult he's becoming rather than just my child, and that I would try to treat him with the respect I'd show anyone.

This ability to observe my own reactions, to step outside the heat of the moment and choose a different response, came largely from reading *The Power of Now*—a secular book that gave me practical tools for managing the legacy of rage I inherited. I don't have to outthink my thinking or change my initial reactions; I must observe them, and in that observation, rationality returns.

———

Internal Family Systems (IFS), or "parts work,"[6] is based on the concept that everyone has multiple internal subpersonalities or "parts." I do parts work with my therapist, John. Developed over 40 years ago by therapist Dick Schwartz while treating adolescents with eating disorders, IFS teaches people to understand and compassionately engage with these different aspects of themselves.

We all carry various internal voices—like an inner critic, worrier or achiever—with some parts dominating our lives while others remain hidden. The goal of IFS is to balance these parts and achieve greater wholeness. The idea is to observe each part of myself with a neutral and open attitude.

A key component involves addressing "exile parts"—aspects

of ourselves that hold painful childhood memories. These exiles often stay buried because it's easier to avoid difficult emotions, but they can resurface during stressful times. Schwartz notes these are often "our most sensitive and loving parts." As it turns out, I have an abundance of love available, and every therapy session is like an excavation.

The healing process requires revisiting and "unburdening" these painful experiences. Schwartz demonstrated this with his childhood shame from his father's criticism, allowing himself to reconnect with that hurt inner child. This process can unlock parts of ourselves that have been suppressed for decades.

My work with John continues and I'm happy to say that I'm making peace with all the parts of me I've identified. Working through so much of my childhood trauma leaves significant room that reveals the depth of love that has always existed within me.

When I felt incapable of loving myself, I assumed I was responsible for all of my pain and all of the ways I ran to avoid that pain. For so long, I thought I did not matter to other people. I tried to assert control in relationships by deploying a destructive type of approach-avoidance that burned more bridges than it built. The closer I moved to a goal—or a person—the stronger both the attraction and the fear became. This would create a "push-pull" dynamic where any movement forward was contrasted by the desire to retreat. I try not to think too long or look too closely at my emotional missteps along the way. I forgive myself where I can.

At the bank, I became a vice president. At church, I became a bishop. I proved to myself that I was capable of succeeding unequivocally. I felt proud that I could push myself to climb such heights, but when I looked around me, I did not truly feel I had achieved what I wanted. But now I know which ladders to climb and I can choose who I want to be my climbing partners, because they are who make the difference.

One rung above me always is my dear wife Karissa. She is

the reason I am able to be fulfilled, not only in the work I do, but in our relationship and roles as parents. Above all else, God is who has remained the steadying force in my life. He placed the right ladders to climb before me, knowing I'd arrive at this particular summit, here and now. I've reached a point where I'm truly happy with my life and I'm surrounded by a loving wife and two incredible children. I've realized that I wouldn't change anything that brought me here, or else I might not have arrived at this place. Therefore, I accept. I accept everything, whether good or evil, that brought me here. I accept them and I accept me.

As I tell my story and work on understanding my past, I'm motivated by the hope that it might help someone else who's experiencing trauma to realize that healing is possible, that it can show them they can climb out of even the deepest, darkest holes and that the journey toward wholeness—while never complete —is always worth taking.

The Japanese concept of *kaizen*—constant improvement— captures what I'm trying to do: to just keep fighting, keep getting a little better each day, keep choosing growth over comfort. There are bluer skies ahead, even when the process to see them is slow and imperfect.

Keep the faith.

O fim.

EPILOGUE

My boots crunch with every step I negotiate in the packed, pristine snow. I pull ahead of our small expedition group, careful to absorb all the beauty surrounding me without causing myself snow blindness. The silence of the tundra has an absolute, almost lethal quality about it—as if a profound hush fell over this untouched world and has never lifted–it's a place of pure untouched beauty, the White Continent, Antarctica.

Each step propels me up a steep incline that sends tiny avalanches of powder behind me. The "hills" we are exploring are solid rock made of compressed ice and snow, eons of history suspended forever in its infinitesimal crystalline structures. The massive icebergs drifting in waters on either side of us look like opulent, iridescent yachts—floating testaments to millions of winters past.

A colony of Adelie penguins waddle up to us without trepidation. Their habitat is so remote, no land predators exist for them to repel, only the very real threat of danger lurking in the water. What freedom they must feel to live without fear.

I reach the summit first, my heart hammering so hard it seems to be generating its own heat. I stand alone on this block of ice, encircled by peaks that scrape the pewter sky. I am surrounded by an ocean that shape-shifts and occupies space so authoritatively, I am humbled and intimidated by its power. The wind whips against my exposed cheeks, causing my eyes to water, which freezes into icicles instantaneously on my skin.

Below me, the water laps against shelves of ice and black volcanic rock. Above, the sky appears close enough for me to touch. I am on the brink of turning 50 years old, standing at the bottom of the world as far away from my childhood home as I ever imagined I would be.

I recall being eight years old, my body pressed against my bedroom window in our cramped, oppressive house, dreaming that someday I might make it all the way to Provo, Utah. "The big city," 150 miles away from our town, might as well have been the distance between me and the moon. Now, here I am, planting my figurative flag like an explorer who has conquered all seven continents. I close my eyes, breathing in the below-freezing air, purified.

Karissa walks up behind me, breathless and grinning. She finds me sitting on a boulder, entranced by the infinite white in front of me. She wraps her arms around me from behind, her embrace warming me from the inside out. I pull her around to face me, her cheeks flush from the cold and the climb. We kiss, the air biting at us, but unable to break through our lips. She holds up her phone to capture this moment, us standing at the edge of everything.

In this moment, I become real. I am the boy who once believed the world began and ended at the desert's limits. I am breathing the rarest air on earth, my heart fractured, yet completely whole.

ACKNOWLEDGMENTS

It's hard to know where to start, because there's no version of this book—or this life—without the people who showed up when I needed them most.

To Karissa: You are the miracle I never saw coming. You gave me love that felt safe, steady and real. You built this life with me —every late night, every risk, every quiet act of faith. Thank you for loving me into the man I am.

To Christian and Victoria: You are the brightest part of my story. Everything I do is so you know what love looks like. I hope you always feel it. I hope you always know it.

To my parents: Thank you for giving me life. However hard and complicated our story has been, I wouldn't be who I am without you.

To my brothers and sisters: Thank you for your strength, your forgiveness and your own stories. I carry you with me always.

To Julie: For helping me get into college, learn how to swim and believe I belonged. Your love changed the course of my life.

To the Edingtons: Thank you for feeding me, housing me, cheering for me and showing me what family can look like when it's built on love.

To Wayne, Keenan and Tammy: Thank you for being my chosen family. You taught me that real love is consistent, not conditional. I carry that with me every day.

To all the amazing friends I've been blessed with along the

way: there are too many of you to name, but please know this: Your kindness, your encouragement and your presence in my life have shaped me more than you know. You've made the hard days easier and the good days even better. I'm so grateful for you.

To the incredible team at Legacy Launch Pad Publishing: Anna, Lucy, Serena and the entire team: Thank you for guiding me through this process with heart, brilliance and grit. This wasn't just a book, it was a reckoning and you helped me do it right.

To John, my therapist: You helped me sit with pain instead of running from it. And in doing that, you helped me find something better than survival: healing.

To my church family: the leaders, teachers, bishops and members who saw something in me and nurtured it with love, patience and truth: Thank you. From my earliest Primary classes to my mission and beyond, you helped me learn what it means to follow Christ and to trust that I was always a child of God, even when I couldn't see it for myself.

To the agents, brokers, partners, and employees at Nuvo Health and across all our agencies: Thank you for being a family. You've shown me that business can be built on trust, integrity, and heart. Thank you for doing what's right, even when it's hard. You inspire me every day to strive for excellence.

To the people who hurt me: I don't thank you for the harm, but I do acknowledge the truth—that walking through what I did gave me the fire to build a life of meaning and purpose.

And to my Heavenly Father and my Savior Jesus Christ: Thank you for loving me through all of it—for staying close when others didn't, for teaching me how to forgive and for guiding me to the life I never thought I could have. I know now that nothing was wasted, and there was no love lost.

This book is proof that you can come from nothing and still choose light. That your past doesn't get to be the final word. And that love—real love—can rewrite everything.

And to you, the reader: Thank you for making space in your life for my story. I hope something in these pages helps you feel less alone and sure of the light ahead.

"If I can stop one heart from breaking, I shall not live in vain."
—Emily Dickinson

BIBLIOGRAPHY

[1] "Black Salve: A Dangerous Corrosive Disguised as an Alternative Medicine" by Andrew J Ordille, Ashley Porter and Amy M Scholl. July 1, 2023.

[2] https://skinwalker-ranch.com/

[3] As told to Nanants, Ruth. (1992). Ute Tales: Coyote Break a Bird's Leg, p. 28. University of Utah Press.

[4] Winters, Jessica. "Screen Time: Motherhood in an age of reproductive surveillance." The New Yorker, April 28, 2025, pp. 54-57.

[5] McCammon, Sarah. The Evangelicals: Loving, Living, and Leaving the White Evangelical Church. (New York, NY, 2024), 4.

[6] Aubrey, Allison. "Ever felt so stressed you didn't know what to do next? Try talking to your 'parts.' NPR, 2024. https://www.npr.org/sections/shots-health-news/2024/10/25/nx-s1-5055753/parts-work-therapy-internal-family-systems-anxiety

ABOUT THE AUTHOR

 Calvin Bagley is a healthcare entrepreneur dedicated to both his family and to demystifying Medicare for millions of Americans. As the founder of Nuvo Health and other ventures, he's helped tens of thousands of individuals navigate healthcare decisions with confidence. Through advocacy efforts in Washington DC, he has also helped reshape the Medicare and health insurance landscape. Beyond championing independent health insurance brokers and investing in healthcare innovation, Bagley is a writer and speaker on leadership and resilience. *Hiding from the School Bus* is his first book.

For more information about Calvin Bagley and *Hiding from the School Bus*, scan the QR code below:

ABOUT THE PUBLISHER

Legacy Launch Pad is a boutique publishing company that works with entrepreneurs from all over the world.

For more information about Legacy Launch Pad Publishing, go to: www.legacylaunchpadpub.com.